Spiritual Identity and Spirit-Empowered Life

Spiritual Identity and Spirit-Empowered Life

Discover Your Identity in God's Family, Purpose in God's Call, and Power in God's Spirit

Thomson K. Mathew

Spiritual Identity and Spirit-Empowered Life

Published by:

GOODNEWS BOOKS
Kottayam, Kerala 686 004, India

ISBN: 1548856835
ISBN 13: 9781548856830

Library of Congress Control Number: 2017911193
CreateSpace Independent Publishing Platform
North Charleston, South Carolina

Praise for *Spiritual Identity and Spirit-Empowered Life*

Because identity theft is so prevalent in today's world, Christians struggle to become empowered by God's Holy Spirit. Dr. Thomson Mathew provides an anointed message on steps for empowerment. Origins, identity, purpose, and rightful living are the keys Dr. Mathew expounds on for obtaining a Spirit-empowered life. Personal examples provide meaningful expression for the one who is seeking more of God's intimacy. This volume is a superb treatise that opens the gate into the power of the Holy Spirit. It is a superb analysis revealing foundational steps for fulfilling one's destiny and a very insightful study providing practical and meaningful illustrations that offer easy application. It is a practical guide to intimacy with God. I highly recommend *Spiritual Identity and Spirit-Empowered Life*.
Dennis Lindsay, D. Min., President, Christ for the Nations, Dallas, Texas

Speaking from a wealth of both pastoral and clinical experience, Dr. Thomson Mathew offers an inspiring yet challenging discussion of spiritual identity and empowerment. As a highly-educated academician, his words carry the ring of authority, and as an accomplished practitioner, they become the voice of hope and healing. Written in a clear and captivating manner, *Spiritual Identity and Spirit-Empowered Life* speaks to an identity crisis within Christian community, and is a must-read for all who want to fulfill their purpose in the power of the Spirit.
William Buker, D. Min., Ph. D., Professor of Christian Counseling, Oral Roberts University, Tulsa, Oklahoma

In this book, Dr. Thomson Mathew, as a theologian, has made the doctrine of Christian living understandable to every Christian by going into the background of Scripture and relating it to us today. He hits the mark of identifying the church then and now. He addresses the church's need to embrace our identity in Christ, walk in our purpose, and live in the power of the Holy Spirit in these last days.

Pastor Sharon Daugherty, Victory Christian Center, Tulsa, Oklahoma

Dr. Thomson K. Mathew addresses a very serious but subtle problem challenging the church in this present day. In his book, *Spiritual Identity and Spirit-Empowered Life,* the core issues of identity, purpose, and power are addressed. Every individual believer must seriously discern what identity means in light of our present culture's attempt to remove any and all boundaries related to historical social norms. In similar fashion, the church is challenged to reevaluate its influence on present day culture and its calling to communicate truth in the midst of a culture that seems determined to redefine truth itself. Finally, Mathew addresses the specific problem of power. The church remains called to represent God's power to a generation that no longer views it as a legitimate source of power. Culture continues to compete with the minds of young people by providing numerous alternatives as valid sources of power. Mathew addresses this reality directly and infers that unless this battle for influence is confronted we will continue to witness a decline in moral standards that reflect the determination of our society in general. He shares candidly what it requires for the church to again exert its influence in tangible and visual ways. This book is a must read if this current culture is to realize the true source of identity, purpose, and power.

Dr. Clarence V. Boyd, Jr., Dean of Spiritual Formation, Oral Roberts University, Tulsa, Oklahoma

This book gives you an opportunity to flesh out who you are in Christ and how you can minister healing to a broken world in your sphere of influence through the power of the Holy Spirit. This book is a timely challenge for all believers both young and old. Dr. Thomson Mathew has challenged all of us to make a greater impact on our world. I encourage you to take this journey with him.

David Wakefield, Ph.D., Licensed Psychologist, Tulsa, Oklahoma

Much like an organ in our body has a purpose for the functioning of our bodies, God has designed you for a specific purpose and has given you the power to thrive in that purpose. Dr. Thomson Mathew beautifully outlines discovering your identity, purpose and power in what God has designed for you. A well written description, based in a solid theological background, *Spiritual Identity and Spirit-Empowered Life* is a must read for any Christian wishing to find a deeper understanding of his or her role on this earth.

Steven B. Katsis, MD, FACS, Past President, Tulsa County Medical Society, Past President, Oklahoma Chapter of the American College of Surgeons, Trauma Surgeon-Police Department Special Operations Team, Tulsa, Oklahoma

Dr. Thomson Mathew's newest book *Spiritual Identity and Spirit-Empowered Life* reveals a path to unlock the potential hidden in every child of God. I had the privilege of meeting this author over twenty-five years ago as he served as a chaplain at the City of Faith Medical Center in Tulsa, Oklahoma. We prayed for patients and witnessed the healing, saving and delivering power of the Holy Spirit. The book is replete with examples that are gleaned from years of ministry. As a nurse and a lay minister I found this book to be practical and theologically sound. The three dimensions of spiritual identity are foundational truths. The heart cry of all believers is to find their purpose in the kingdom of God and to harness the power of the Holy Spirit to accomplish that purpose. This book answers these concerns and is an excellent resource for personal spiritual growth. The questions at the end of each chapter serve as a tool that can also be used for Bible studies or in a group/classroom setting. It is my pleasure to recommend this book to all Christians in the marketplace.

Adeline Barber, RN MSN OCN CCM, Cancer Treatment Center, Tulsa, Oklahoma

Dr. Thomson Mathew focuses on three essential areas that empower Christians to fulfill their God given potential, which are understanding who they are in Christ, understanding their calling, and understanding their authority to execute that calling. Theologically sound from a Charismatic perspective, this easy-to-read book is an excellent tool for chaplains to use for various audiences at Bible studies/fellowship groups, during pastoral counseling sessions, or even for their own personal spiritual development.

Chaplain (Major) Pinkie Fischer, U.S. Army Chaplain Corps

Contents

Introduction

In my work as a pastor, chaplain, and seminary professor, I have come across many individuals who struggle with significant life issues and live with much pain because of a lack of identity and purpose in their lives. As a college dean, I have seen many students struggling with their calling and purpose, and professors who have been concerned about their students' lack of spiritual identity. I have met individuals with similar issues outside the field of education also, in churches, ministries, and marketplaces, living unfulfilled lives, engaging in unhealthy practices, falling down in their walk with God on a regular basis, and failing to fulfill their potential. They are trying very hard but are unable to live a whole-person life in this broken world in spite of the power that is available to them to live that way.

Pastoral conversations with some of these Christian brothers and sisters have shown me that the root of the problem in many cases is a lack of understanding of who they really are, especially as spiritual beings. Psychologists have already established that self-identity is a key to success in life,[1] but we often associate the challenge of identity as a problem in adolescence, not in adulthood. Knowing who we are is important at all stages of life, but knowing who we are in God because of the life, death, and resurrection of Jesus, and what God thinks of us because of Him, is even more vital. I am convinced that one's spiritual identity—knowing and incorporating and living out of who one really is as a Spirit-empowered Christian—is more important than any other identity, national, economic, or racial. I am convinced that it is impossible for a person to reach his full potential until he knows and accepts who he really is as a Spirit-empowered Christian, not in some superficial or sloganized way, but in a deep and soul-penetrating way.

Successful life and ministry and fulfillment of one's calling and purpose—no matter what it is—depend on spiritual power. The empowerment for a purposeful life is maximized only when one incorporates his or her true spiritual identity into his or her innermost being.

This we learn from Jesus Christ. Jesus accomplished His mission fully because He was able to overcome the challenges to His identity that came His way regularly from high and low places. His "I am" statements in the gospel of John give clear evidence of this (John 6:35; 10:9; 14:6). In *Jesus the Pastor*,[2] teaching pastor John W. Frye identified the characteristics of Jesus that em-

---

1 David Sortino, "Creating a Success Identity," *Press Democrat*, March 23, 2012, n.p., http://davidsortino.blogs.pressdemocrat.com/10116/creating-a-success-identity/.

2 John W. Frye, *Jesus the Pastor: Leading Others in the Character and Power of Christ* (Grand Rapids: Zondervan, 2000), 50–54.

powered Him to fulfill His destiny. Frye pointed out that Jesus had a strong sense of identity; He knew who He was and what He was called to do. This sense of identity enabled Him to focus on His destiny and purpose. Significantly, Jesus did not depend on His ministerial performance to settle His identity; His Father had affirmed Him long before He performed His first miracle, saying "You are my Son, whom I love; with you I am well pleased" (Luke 3:22). Jesus' identity was not performance-based; rather it was rooted in God the Father. Many Christians fall into the trap of performance-based identity, but a biblical model of Spirit-empowered Christian identity is anchored in God, our relationship to Him, His purposes for our lives, and the empowerment of the Holy Spirit.

Jesus went about doing His Father's work because He knew who He was. He was not afraid of the devil, although he took the power of evil seriously. He took authority over the devil based on His identity. He knew that He was the Son of God and that the Spirit of the Lord was upon Him (Luke 4:18).

Erik Erikson, the noted psychologist, has conducted significant research in the area of youth and identity. After studying all the stages of human life and the unique problems of each stage, Erikson concluded that the most significant issue for young people is the question of identity.[3] I agree with him but am also convinced that the issue of identity is not limited to adolescence. It is a lifelong issue, and the question of spiritual identity is even more crucial for all ages.

---

3 Erik H. Erikson, *Identity: Youth in Crisis* (New York: W. W. Norton & Co, 1968), 88-91.

Technology and globalization have brought us the fear of identity theft. Many of us have taken measures to prevent it. However, the loss of identity, particularly spiritual identity, remains a real threat to Christians today. This book is a sincere effort to help Christians guard against it.

Based on my study of the Bible and experiences in preaching, teaching, and counseling Christians of all ages for more than three decades, I present fifteen streams within three dimensions (identity, purpose, and power) of a Christian's spiritual identity in this book. Each chapter presents one stream. You will encounter the following truths in this volume, each forming a thread of Spirit-empowered Christian identity. Think of these as biblical windows to the heart of God concerning your true identity.

1. You are a Child of God
2. You are a Member of God's Family
3. You are a Disciple of Jesus Christ
4. You are a Citizen of the Kingdom of God
5. You are a Whole Person, by Faith
6. You are a Healer, Serving a Wounded Healer
7. You are a Believer, Worshipper, and Hope-Bearer
8. You are a Leader
9. You are a Missionary
10. You are a Prophet
11. You are a Temple, not the Taj Mahal
12. You are a Gifted Person
13. You are a Blessed Person

14. You are a Saint, Now
15. You are an Anointed Person, Empowered to Fulfill Your Purpose

I want every follower of Jesus to know that a Christian is one who has been born again into a new identity, which he or she must discover and incorporate. Every Christian has been adopted into God's family. He or she is an heir of the Father and a joint-heir with Jesus Christ and has the privilege of calling the almighty God by the familiar term *Abba* (Father). This is the basis of all other facets of our spiritual identity.

I recommend reading this book slowly, taking the time to reflect on one chapter at a time. At the end of each chapter, reflect on the questions I have included and ask the Lord to let you incorporate the truth contained in that chapter. My prayer is that you will be able to deeply comprehend and fully incorporate all the components of your spiritual identity into your mind and spirit and be able to walk in that knowledge with the help of the Holy Spirit. I want the enemy to be afraid of you as you reach your full potential and fulfill your destiny.

This book is also meant to be a resource to be shared in a group context to encourage dialogue among believers. We live in a world that is constantly telling Christians who they should be. We must learn to define ourselves by how the Holy Spirit sees us.

I am writing this during a generous sabbatical approved as part of my transition back to professorship after sixteen years of service as dean of the College of Theology and Ministry at

Oral Roberts University. I wish to express my sincere gratitude to President William M. Wilson and Provost Kathleen Reid Martinez. I also wish to extend my thanks to the faculty and staff that stood with me as a strong team for such a long time, and especially during major institutional transitions. I want to acknowledge the support and assistance I have received in multiple ways from the following individuals: my wife Molly; my children Amy and Fiju Koshy and Jamie Mathew; Judy Cope, who served as my administrative assistant for nearly two decades; Marlene Mankins, a capable editorial assistant; and dean's fellow Heather Wright.

I wish you God's very best as you read these pages.

Thomson K. Mathew

Prologue

Jesus, Paul, and You

In the book of Acts, which contains the serious story of the first-century church, we come across an at once sad and humorous incident in chapter 19. This unexpected event shows the importance of having a strong and authentic Christian spiritual identity. It also emphasizes the importance of having a *Spirit-empowered* Christian identity.

Paul the apostle was in Ephesus, where he met some disciples, about twelve men. They had been baptized by John's baptism, they said. John had baptized them in the name of Jesus, so they were not familiar with the Holy Spirit. Paul laid hands on them and they received the Holy Spirit.

Paul ministered in and around Ephesus for about two years, preaching, teaching, and healing. "God did extraordinary miracles through Paul, so that even handkerchiefs and aprons that had touched him were taken to the sick, and their illnesses were cured and the evil spirits left them" (Acts 19:11–12). Many were blessed by Paul's ministry there and believed in Jesus. Others did not accept Christ but were fascinated by the supernatural elements of his ministry and their impact on people. Desiring similar effects on people and seeking the results Paul had in his ministry, some tried to imitate him.

There was a Jewish chief priest named Sceva who had seven sons. These men tried to imitate Paul in a real-life situation and attempted to cast out an evil spirit from a possessed man by saying, "In the name of Jesus whom Paul preaches, I command you to come out." Seeing nothing happening, they kept repeating the same command. Finally, the evil spirit spoke to them, saying, "Jesus I know, and I know about Paul, but who are you?" They were startled, but that was not the end. Now comes the sad—and humorous—part of the story: "Then the man who had the evil spirit jumped on them and overpowered them all. He gave them such a beating that they ran out of the house naked and bleeding" (Acts 19:13–16)!

God has not called us to a naked and bleeding life or ministry. We are not supposed to be beaten up by the enemy. The enemy beats up people who do not have a strong and positive spiritual identity.

The evil spirit told the sons of Sceva that he knew Jesus and Paul, but had no clue who *they* were. In other words, this spirit recognized the identities and the authority of Jesus and His apostle Paul, but he questioned the identities and authority of these people, because they lacked any identity that represented a relationship with Jesus and a connection to the power of the Holy Spirit.

One's spiritual identity represents one's authority and power. Jesus had to face the question of identity on a regular basis. People constantly challenged His identity. "Is this not the carpenter's son?" they asked. "His mother and brothers are among us," they said (Matt. 13:55, paraphrased). In other words, they were trying to ascertain His identity as the source of His authority and power, but His identity was not limited to who His earthly father was or who His mother and brothers were. It was more comprehensive, taking into account not only His earthly family connections but also His spiritual relationships. Jesus' identity and authority were connected to more sources than His biological roots.

Recall the time when Jesus asked His disciples, "Who do people say the Son of Man is?" They replied, "Some say John the Baptist; others say Elijah; and still others, Jeremiah or one of the prophets." "But what about you?" Jesus asked, narrowing the focus of His question. "Who do you say I am?" Peter replied on behalf of all of them, "You are the Messiah, the Son of the living God." Jesus then told them that it was not flesh and blood that had revealed this truth to them, but His Father in heaven (Matt. 16:13–17). It was a revelation. Jesus wanted them to know His true identity and its horizontal and vertical dimensions.

Jesus knew who He was. This is confirmed again and again in the biblical record. He said:

1. "I am the way, the truth and the life." (John 14:6)
2. "I am the gate." (John 10:9)
3. "I am the light of the world." (John 8:12)

4. "I am the living bread that came down from heaven." (John 6:51)
5. "I am the good shepherd." (John 10:11)
6. "I am the vine." (John 15:5)
7. "I am the Alpha and the Omega." (Rev. 1:8)

Jesus had a strong identity. His identity was not based on His performance. As I wrote in the introduction, He was already affirmed by His Father before His first miracle. His identity was rooted in God the Father. It was naturally connected to His earthly relationships, but transcending those, it was rooted deeply in His relationship with His heavenly Father, who had given Him His purpose and destiny, and in the power of the Spirit that was upon Him (Luke 4:18).

Remember the time when Jesus entered Jerusalem and the people asked, "Who is this?" He had been there many times, but it seems that the Holy One was unknown in the holy city. Jesus did not verbally answer their question that day; instead He went into the temple and began to heal the sick. He was answering the question of His identity with His deeds rather than His words. He demonstrated that He was the One with divine authority over the temple. He was not the priest or the high priest, but He was the One with authority to cleanse the temple. The blind and the lame came in when Jesus was in the temple, but they did not leave blind or lame. That was the demonstration of His identity and authority; that was His answer to the question, "Who is this?"

Jesus knew who He was. His identity empowered Him to fulfill His purpose and destiny. Knowing who He was and empowered by that knowledge and the anointing of the Holy Spirit, He exercised authority over natural forces, demonic powers, sicknesses, and death (Luke 8). The devil knew that Jesus was the Son of God. He knew that all authority had been given to Jesus. The people missed it on that day in Jerusalem because He had come riding on a donkey. But the devil did not miss it, and that is clear from the evil spirit's response to the sons of Sceva.

Like Jesus, Paul also had a strong sense of identity. The devil knew him too. Paul's identity gave him and represented in him the authority of an apostle. He talked about being "circumcised on the eighth day, of the people of Israel, of the tribe of Benjamin, a Hebrew of Hebrews; in regard to the law, a Pharisee; as for zeal, persecuting the church; as for righteousness based on the law, faultless" (Phil 3:5–6). He had a very strong ethnic identity based on his family and his accomplishments, but while owning that personal identity, he counted all of it a loss and embraced instead his spiritual identity. He knew that he was an apostle, called, empowered, and sent by God. He did not apologize for it, but his spiritual identity gave him the authority to say to others without fear, "I charge you" (1 Thess. 5:27; 1 Tim. 5:21; 6:13), "I exhort you" (Acts 27:22 KJV), and "Who has bewitched you?" (Gal. 3:1). This strong sense of spiritual identity was behind his supernatural ministry in Ephesus, which the sons of Sceva disastrously tried to imitate.

The chief priest's sons ran into trouble by not being followers of Jesus in an authentic way. They were not filled with the Holy Spirit, so they were missing the empowerment they needed to cast the spirit out. The evil spirit wound up questioning their identity and overcoming them physically. They had to run for their lives, bleeding and naked.

Spiritual identity matters. Having a strong sense of identity as a member of God's family and a vessel of the Holy Spirit is very important to living a purposeful and victorious Christian life. To live as a whole person in a broken world requires one to have a strong spiritual identity. This book is about discovering, developing, and living out our Spirit-empowered Christian identity. As mentioned in the introduction, I have discovered in God's Word fifteen threads or streams of our spiritual identity, which I will present in three categories (dimensions) in this book. Primarily, the first five deal with our identity in relation to God's family; the second group presents our identity in terms of God's purposes for our lives; the third category describes our identity as it relates to the empowerment of the Holy Spirit. Each thread or stream of our spiritual identity represents its own corresponding authority and power granted to us by the Word of God. Together they form a great force within us, like multiple streams becoming a mighty river. This Spirit-driven force enables each of us to live a purposeful life with a whole-person lifestyle and to impact the world in a positive way.

Read each chapter and reflect on its content in light of your own life. Consider the biblical references and respond to the questions at the end of each chapter. Keep a prayerful attitude as you join me in this journey. May you be impacted by what you are about to encounter.

Part 1

Discovering Your Identity in God's Family

Chapter 1

△ △ △

You Are a Child of God

*But as many as received Him, to them He
gave the right to become children of God,
to those who believe in His name.*

—JOHN 1:12 NKJV

A Hindu man in India, upset about his son becoming a
Christian, rushed into a church service with some hired
members of a local gang and attacked the pastor and other worshippers. Seeing his father beating up his pastor, the young con-
vert jumped up to protect his shepherd but was hit in the face
by a gang member. Suddenly the scene changed as the father
turned on the gang member who had hit his son and punched
him out!

The Hindu man did not appreciate his son's conversion to Christianity, but the boy was still his son, and this father did not want him to get hurt. There is something special about fathers and sons, even imperfect ones. The Bible tells us that we are sons and daughters of a perfect Father, God (John 1:12; Rom. 8:14–16; also Matt. 5:48)!

Yes, you are a child of God. Let's begin this study of our spiritual identity by reflecting on this profound truth.

The formation of one's self-identity is an essential part of every person's development. In the introduction, I mentioned the findings of psychoanalyst Erik Erikson, who concluded that the question of identity is critical among young people. However, in my work with individuals both young and old, I have discovered that the question of identity is, in fact, a vital issue to people of *all* ages. Many grown-ups, including sincere Christians, do not know their true identity.

Unfortunately, various cults and fringe groups take advantage of this lack of solid identity. It is sad to see individuals who lack a true sense of identity turn foolishly to disempowering cults, dehumanizing gangs, Far Eastern religions, and violent jihads of the Middle East to find their identity and purpose. The question of identity is behind a lot of the problems we encounter both in individuals' lives and in society.

It is God's will for us to know who we are in Him. Our authentic identity is found in God, our Creator. As Christians, our true identity is our spiritual identity, and it begins with our status as children of God. The concept of God as Father is strong in the Old Testament, but Jesus of Nazareth brought the idea to its fullest clarity through His life, death, and resurrection.

As a Christian, you are a child of God. When I served as a seminary dean at Oral Roberts University, I made it a habit to read the doctoral dissertations of new theology professors we hired. I wanted to know the areas of their research and the quality of their academic work. The dissertations gave me the best evidences of their scholarship. Some of them were very deep and dealt with topics that were hard to grasp, especially when the volumes contained texts in multiple languages. One of the impressive ones I read belonged to Dr. Edward Watson, who earned his PhD in New Testament at Baylor University. Basically, his entire treatise was on one biblical concept: adoption, the word Saint Paul used to communicate the idea that we as Gentiles have been embraced by God and included in His family (see Rom. 8:15 et al.).

The most notable discovery for me in Watson's dissertation was the fact that under Greco-Roman law, with which Paul was very familiar, a man could disown and disinherit his biological son, but could not do so with an adopted son. I was moved by the idea that Paul chose the word *adoption* to describe how we got into God's family and became His sons and daughters. We are children of God, and our standing in God's family is an amazing story. Look at what the Scriptures have to say about our new status:

> But as many as received him, to them gave he the power
> to become the sons of God, even to them that believe on
> his name. (John 1:12 KJV)

> The Spirit himself testifies with our spirit that we are God's children. Now if we are children, then we are heirs—heirs of God and co-heirs with Christ. (Rom. 8:16–17)
>
> Dear friends, now we are children of God. (1 John 3:2)

What a privilege it is to know that, as Christians, we are God's offspring on earth. May this knowledge be always upon our hearts and minds, and may each of us always be able to say, "I am a child of God!"

This identity does not make us proud and boastful. Christians must celebrate their identity as children of God, but never assume that they are somehow superior to their fellow human beings. We are, of course, children of God, and yet we remain sinners saved purely by the grace of God, not by any effort or merit on our part. The apostle Paul was always conscious of his status as a saved sinner or, more precisely, a saved former sinner. He wrote to Timothy, "Here is a trustworthy saying that deserves full acceptance: Christ Jesus came into the world to save sinners—of whom I am the worst. But for that very reason I was shown mercy so that in me, the worst of sinners, Christ Jesus might display his immense patience as an example for those who would believe in him and receive eternal life" (1 Tim. 1:15–16). Paul also reminded the Christians at Ephesus of their status as sinners saved only by grace and through faith: "For it is by grace you have been saved, through faith—and this is not from yourselves, it is the gift of God—not by works, so that no one can boast" (Eph. 2:8–9).

The essence of the good news, or the gospel, is that we have been given the power to become sons and daughters of God. In this first chapter, let's look at the key elements of the good news to see the bigger picture.

God loves this world. The Bible tells us that God loves the world (John 3:16). He loves it with an unconditional love. The word used to describe God's love, *agape*, means totally unconditional, unmerited love. Human love can be characterized as "if" love and "because of" love, but God's love is "in spite of" love. In spite of what we may have done in the past, in spite of our background, God loves us. He is able to do this because, according to His Word, He *is* love (1 John 4:7–8).

Jesus presented God as a loving Father. He called him "Abba, Father" (Mark 14:36). In the parable of the prodigal son (Luke 15:11–32), the father is portrayed as a loving, kind, and patient person. He represents God. While many people visualize God as an angry and authoritarian monarch, the New Testament portrays a God who is *agape*.

It is true that humankind has disobeyed God and His creation has rebelled against Him. It is also true that we have broken God's heart through our sinful ways. But God has not stopped loving us. He still loves His world. He loves us. This is good news, as are the following evidences of God's love for us:

God sent His Son. "For God so loved the world that he gave his one and only Son," says John 3:16. The good news means that God not only loved this world, but He expressed that love for all to see by sending His Son Jesus into the world. Love is not true love until it is expressed. God expressly manifested His love toward us by sending His Son to our world. Giving up the glory of heaven, Jesus came to us in the form of a man and revealed the Father's immeasurable love for us.

God had revealed His love for us through various means throughout human history. According to the Bible, however, God ultimately and fully revealed Himself to us in and through His Son, Jesus. The Word became flesh in Jesus (John 1:14). We saw the glory of the Father on the face of His Son Jesus Christ.

Jesus revealed not only God's love for us, but also His will for us—that no one should perish, but should have everlasting life (John 3:16). This required a supreme sacrifice. The Bible tells us that Jesus became that sacrifice for all humankind. He gave His life on a cross at a place called Calvary so that humanity would require no more sacrifices for forgiveness, salvation, and adoption into God's family. Human beings only need to believe in the once-and-for-all sacrifice of Jesus. This, indeed, is good news.

"Whoever *believes* in him shall not perish but have eternal life," the Bible says (John 3:16, emphasis added). What great news! Many, unfortunately, are still trying to earn their salvation by offering up their own sacrifices. No such requirement exists. This may sound unbelievable and even foolish, but the only requirement is that we believe in Jesus. He paid our debt. He died in our place. He still offers salvation, full and free. This salvation turns out to be an adoption. By believing in Jesus, we become sons and daughters of God. This is remarkable.

Jesus is still alive. The story of Jesus does not end in a borrowed tomb. The Bible goes on to say that though He died on Calvary and was buried in a borrowed tomb, He was raised from the dead on the third day. After the resurrection, He was seen by many and was later taken up to heaven. We are told that He is now seated at the right hand of His Father, interceding for us (see John 20–21; Acts 1:3, 9–10; 13:30–31; Col. 3:1; Heb. 7:24–25).

The risen Christ sent the Holy Spirit to our world (John 15:26). Those who accept Christ are born of the Spirit. This new birth is the adoption Paul is discussing in his epistles.

> The Spirit you received does not make you slaves, so that you live in fear again; rather, the Spirit you received brought about your adoption to sonship. And by him we cry, *"Abba,* Father." (Rom. 8:15)
>
> He predestined us for adoption to sonship through Jesus Christ, in accordance with his pleasure and will. (Eph. 1:5)

The Spirit not only makes us sons and daughters of God, but leads us and guides us to do God's will to fulfill His purposes in the world. We have been adopted with a purpose. Life in the Spirit is a life of purpose, victory, and power.

We live in a world of dead heroes and are surrounded by many leaders. The followers of Jesus do not follow a dead leader; they follow the living Christ. Jesus is alive today, and, according to the Bible, we as the children of God live and move and have our being in Him (Acts 17:28).

Jesus is coming again. We live in a world where hope is a rare commodity. Despair is seen around the world. Human problems are countless, and many people are at their wits' end. In this dark horizon, there is a silver lining called Christian hope. It is the promise that Jesus Christ is coming again. The Bible contains more promises about the second coming of Christ than about His first.

The hope provided by the life, death, and resurrection of Jesus has removed the fear of death from His followers. They no longer live with the fear of the grave, as they know that because He lives, they shall live also (John 14:19). Only a Christian can exclaim, "O death, where is thy sting? O grave, where is thy victory?" (1 Cor. 15:55 KJV).

Our ultimate hope is not built on any material thing. It is not in a particular government or system. Our hope is in a person, the person of the Lord Jesus Christ. He is our hope, our only hope. According to the Bible, one of these days, the children of God will be gathered together from all tribes and nations of earth (Rev. 7:9). A glorious gathering of the children of God has been announced. What a day that will be! We can only imagine the unspeakable joy we will experience on that day! This is good news.

We are children of the promises. It is not a small thing to claim that we are God's children. When we do so, we are claiming that we are already heirs of God, coheirs with Jesus Christ, and inheritors of God's promises. It is hard to comprehend this truth because we are a generation of promise breakers. We are so used to broken promises that we are no longer surprised when they go unfulfilled. Manufacturers, employers, and politicians routinely break promises. Husbands and wives and fathers and mothers can't seem to keep them either, and our hearts are broken. Then we find out that God our Father is a promise *giver* and we don't know how to process that information. We don't know if we can believe His promises.

We don't know how to handle promises such as "I will never leave you"; "I am the LORD who heals you"; or "Ask and it will be given to you; seek and you will find; knock and the door will be opened to you" (Heb. 13:5 NKJV; Ex. 15:26 NKJV; Matt. 7:7). We seem to think—maybe secretly and unconsciously—that God is like us: a promise breaker. But Paul the apostle disagrees with us. He says, "For no matter how many promises God has made, they are 'Yes' in Christ. And so through him the 'Amen' is spoken by us to the glory of God" (2 Cor. 1:20). Missionary E. Stanley Jones, in his last book, *The Divine Yes*, agreed with Paul, writing that Jesus is the yes of God to us.[4] All of God's promises are "yes" in Jesus Christ to those who are His children.

You may have heard the story of the old beggar who was given a large check by someone who had known him in his youth. He was afraid to take the check to the bank because of the way he looked, fearing that he would be accused of theft. But when he got to the bank, he was told that the check would be honored because of the one who signed it, not because of the appearance of the one who had presented it. God's promises are good because God is God and He is good. They will be fulfilled because God is the giver of them, and He is a promise keeper. You are

---

4 E. Stanley Jones, *The Divine Yes* (Nashville: Abingdon, 1975).

not a beggar in the sight of God. You are His child. Your claims are valid.

God's Word is a book of promises. We often miss the promises of God, just like the poor son who never opened the Bible his mother had given him many years earlier that contained many active promissory notes. We need to know the promises of God and actualize them. God will keep the promises He has offered to us in His Word because of Jesus and because we are His beloved children. The key words in 2 Corinthians 1:20 are "in Christ": "For no matter how many promises God has made, they are 'Yes' *in Christ*" (emphasis added).

God's promises will be fulfilled in your life because they are attached to God's purposes for your life. There are no co-incidences with God. The arrival of the Midianites at Joseph's pit was not just a coincidence (Gen. 37:28). Pharaoh's daughter being at the Nile when baby Moses was hidden near the bank was not an accident (Ex. 2:5). The young maid being employed at Commander Naaman's house was not accidental (2 Kings 5:2ff). The king's inability to fall asleep, which caused him to read a book of chronicles that recorded how Mordecai had saved his life, was not just a fluke (Esth. 6:1–3). The boy picking up five smooth stones from the brook was not just a bored teenager (1 Sam. 17:40). God was fulfilling His purposes in and through these people. He was keeping His promises.

God is concerned about us, His sons and daughters. He bought us with the blood of His only Son and wants to give us every good thing. Romans 8:32 asks, "He who did not spare his own Son, but gave him up for us all—how will he not also, along with him, graciously give us all things?"

Look at the Old Testament promises He has already fulfilled. Abraham did become a blessing to the nations, just as God promised (Gen. 22:17). The earth has not been destroyed by flood since Noah's time (Gen. 9:11). The people of Israel are not slaves in Egypt anymore (Ex. 3:7–10). Our sons and daughters are now prophesying, as God promised through the prophet Joel (Joel 2:28).

The New Testament bears the same witness of God's promise-keeping power. He has promised to save us, heal us, empower us, sustain us, provide for us, guide us, and never leave us (Heb. 7:25; Ex. 15:26; Acts 1:8; 2 Cor. 1:3–4; Ps. 32:8; John 14:18). He is fulfilling these promises now. He has promised to build His church in such a way that the gates of hell will never destroy it (Matt. 16:18). I see Him doing that now around the world. I have no doubt that He will keep the remaining great promises also, including the ultimate one made by Jesus, "I will come again" (John 14:3 NKJV).

All God's promises belong to us as His children. All of them will be fulfilled because of Jesus Christ our Lord and Savior. I encourage you to internalize your identity as a child of God at a deeper level and begin to claim His promises.

You are not only born of the Spirit, but also filled with the Spirit. Being filled with the Spirit adds a deeper dimension to your spiritual identity. I invite you to consider your identity as a Spirit-filled Christian and contemplate its deeper implications.

My daughter Elizabeth Mathew Koshy, PhD, who is a professional psychologist, helped me to grasp this concept better using three biblical images. She believes that Spirit-filled Christians are people defined by fire. As the image of fire is used to represent the Holy Spirit throughout the Bible, Elizabeth points out three aspects of a Spirit-filled identity that relate to this imagery:

1. The Spirit-filled identity includes moments when we *call down* fire.
2. The Spirit-filled identity includes moments when we *walk through* fire.
3. The Spirit-filled identity includes a lifestyle of *carrying* the fire with us.

Let me explain this perspective.

Calling down fire. First Kings 18:16-39 relates Elijah's challenge to the prophets of Baal on top of Mount Carmel. During this encounter, Elijah proposes that the 450 prophets of Baal show physical evidence that their god is real by giving them the opportunity to call fire down from heaven and burn up a bull. The prophets call on Baal for hours, dancing, shouting, even inflicting self-injury, but nothing happens. They receive no response from Baal. It is now Elijah's turn.

First Elijah sets up an altar, places the bull on top of it, and drowns it with water three times. Then he loudly declares that the God of Abraham, Isaac, and Jacob is God of all. Immediately, fire falls from heaven, consuming the entire sacrifice, water, and bull (vv. 16–39). The charismatic experience is full of mountaintop moments when we have the privilege of "calling down fire" and seeing God's power manifest itself right before our eyes even today. This is an important part (and the most popular part) of what it means to be Spirit-filled. But this is not the only part of the Spirit-filled Christian identity.

Walking through fire. In Daniel 3:13-30 we read of three brave God-followers, Shadrach, Meshach, and Abednego, who refuse to follow King Nebuchadnezzar's decree and worship false gods. As a result of their decision, they are punished by being thrown into a blazing furnace, a sure death by human standards. The young men stated that they knew God was able to save them, but even if He chose not to, they would not worship other gods. They walked into the fire believing they were alone. But God had another plan in mind.

In verse 25, we read that there was a *fourth* man in the fire. God's own presence went with Shadrach, Meshach, and Abednego as they walked through fire for what they believed in. They left the furnace unharmed, giving all glory to God (vv. 13–30).

A true Spirit-filled Christian identity requires a willingness to discard our own lives for the sake of God's truth, remembering that as we "walk through fire," our God is with us.

Carrying the fire with us. Finally, the most important aspect of a Spirit-filled Christian identity is found in what most people would consider one of the least important biblical characters. In Luke 2:36-38 we learn of a woman by the name of Anna. She was an elderly prophetess who had been widowed for eighty-four years. Every day she was at the temple, fasting and praying.

When we think about the cultural context in which this was written, Anna was a person of no value in her society. She had no male representation. She had no children that we are aware of. She was seen as socially invisible. Yet, she worshipped day and night (vv. 36–38). Take a moment to imagine this scene: an older woman, ignored by society, daily saying these words in the temple: "My Messiah is coming." I can hear her now. "My Messiah is coming." Can you see the others in the synagogue barely tolerating her? In spite of her low estate and poor social status, we find this woman, Anna, saying, "My Messiah is coming."

In a moment, after more than eighty years of loneliness and disempowerment, Anna looks up and recognizes her Savior—in the form of an infant in the arms of Mary and Joseph—gives gratitude to God, and immediately begins telling those around her who Jesus is. This is the core of Spirit-filled Christian experience.

Fast-forward with me to the book of Acts (also written by Luke). In Acts 1:8, Jesus appears post-resurrection to His disciples, with this promise, "You will receive power when the Holy Spirit comes on you; and you will be my witnesses in Jerusalem, and in all Judea and Samaria, and to the ends of the earth."

"Carrying the fire with us" means that in this world full of pain and emptiness, we have the faith, like Anna, to see Jesus for who He is (regardless of the social pressure to do otherwise). We also have the gratitude and humility, like Anna, to recognize the gift of salvation. And like those who were in the Upper Room (Acts 2), as a result of the coming of the Holy Spirit, we have an internal "burning" to share who Jesus is with others, not just in our immediate influence, but far beyond.

Spiritual identity has three dimensions: identity, purpose, and power. The first thread (stream) of our identity as Christians is our status as sons and daughters of God. A Spirit-empowered Christian identity undergirds this notion. "Spirit-empowered spiritual identity" refers to a life defined by calling down fire, walking through fire, and ultimately carrying the fire with us wherever we go.

So I conclude this chapter with a reminder: You are a child of God. You are a son or a daughter of God. You have the fire of the Holy Spirit within you. Walk in the power of your identity as a child of God, daring to call down fire when needed, trusting to walk through fire when required, and carrying the fire within you always. As you go, claim the promises of God for you and your household in the name of Jesus Christ.

Questions for Reflection

1. What does the term "child of God" mean to you?
2. What are your thoughts on the concept of adoption as the way we have become sons and daughters of God?
3. What are the five aspects of the "Good News" presented in this chapter?
4. What is the connection between being a child of God and fulfilling the purposes of God?
5. Have you thought about your identity as a child of God and God's purpose for your life?
6. What are some of the Old Testament promises God has fulfilled?
7. What are some of the New Testament promises God has fulfilled (or is fulfilling)?
8. How does Elizabeth Mathew Koshy connect the concept of *fire* with her Spirit-filled Christian identity?
9. What concept in this chapter speaks to you personally?
10. How would you assess the strength of your identity as a child of God?

Chapter 2

You are a Member of God's Family

"Can a mother forget the baby at her breast, and have no compassion on the child she has borne? Though she may forget, I will not forget you! See, I have engraved you on the palms of my hands; your walls are ever before me."

—Isaiah 49:15–16

The parable of the good Samaritan is one of the best-known stories in the world. Jesus used it to help us discover the answer to the question, "Who is my neighbor?" Curiously, Jesus did not give us a parable to answer the question, "Who is my family?" I wonder if it is because His whole life was a parable answering that question.

The words for *family* in the Old Testament (*bayit* in Hebrew) and New Testament (*oikos* in Greek) mean "house" or "household." The Old Testament concept of household included extended family and even employees, who could be servants or slaves. Even employed aliens and guests could be considered part of the household in the Old Testament. The New Testament idea of household was not much different, as it also included extended family, employees, and others involved with them. A typical Old Testament family could include more than fifty members. Jacob's family seemed to have at least seventy members (Gen. 46:5–27). This is a far cry from modern concepts of family. It is not easy for people belonging to current nuclear families to appreciate the full meaning of family in the Word of God.

In Old Testament times one's identity was based on one's family. The Bible teaches that family was God's idea, and the Maker of heaven and earth Himself created the first family (Gen. 2:19–24). The laws of the old covenant protected the family and provided rules of conduct regarding the family.[5] Family was blessed by God, and children were considered a blessing (Ps. 127:3–5). Barrenness was considered a curse, so incidents of barren women receiving children were highlighted in the community's stories (1 Sam.2:5). Sarah, the patriarch Isaac's mother, and Hannah, the prophet Samuel's mother, were Old Testament stars.

---

5 For a short but comprehensive survey on family in the Bible, see Brenda B. Colijn, "Family in the Bible: A Brief Survey," *Ashland Theological Journal* 36 (2004): 73–84., https://biblicalstudies.org.uk/pdf/ashland_theological_ journal/36–1_073.pdf.

The God of the Old Testament worked in and through families. He was involved in Abraham's family and David's household. He was unhappy with Eli's and Saul's families. The Old Testament presents God as both a father (Deut. 32:6; Isa. 64:8) and a mother (Isa. 66:13). He is Israel's father (Jer. 31:9), and Israel is His firstborn (Ex. 4:22). He pities like a father (Ps. 103:13) but protects His children like a mother (Hos. 13:8). He chastises His children as a father does, but trains His offspring as a mother eagle does (Deut. 32:11–12 KJV). God is a providing father and a caring and sustaining mother. He is also portrayed as a husband (Jer. 31:32) and a provider (Gen. 22:14).

The New Testament also presents a very positive portrait of family and provides guidelines for Christian family life. Jesus paid attention to parents and responded to their pleas on behalf of their children. He healed Jairus's daughter (Mark 5:22–24, 38–42) and the Syrophoenician woman's daughter (Mark 7:24–30). He raised the son of the widow of Nain from the dead (Luke 7:11–17). He blessed the little children who were brought to Him and rebuked the disciples for forbidding them (Luke 18:16). He affirmed marriage and taught against divorce (Matt. 19:3–12).

The New Testament gives much information regarding the family of Jesus, and pays attention to His long heritage. He is the son of David. Both Matthew and Luke list elaborate genealogies to establish His lineage, Luke's being more extended (Matt. 1:1–17; Luke 3:23–38). We read there that Jesus is the seed of Abraham and He belongs to the household of David (Luke 1:69; 2:4).

The fatherhood of God was revealed more fully by Jesus. As the Word became flesh and lived among us, God became "Abba." Jesus used the parable of the lost son to teach about God's fatherhood. His listeners learned that God is a loving Father who patiently waits for His children to return to Him.

We know more about Paul's Christian community than about his immediate family, but the apostle Paul made considerable effort to protect the ideal of a Christian family. He showed special concern and respect for older women and widows. See his advice to Timothy: "But if a widow has children or grandchildren, these should learn first of all to put their religion into practice by caring for their own family and so repaying their parents and grandparents, for this is pleasing to God" (1 Tim. 5:4). He added, "If any woman who is a believer has widows in her care, she should continue to help them and not let the church be burdened with them, so that the church can help those widows who are really in need" (5:16).

Paul was tough on men who would not provide for their families. He discounted their faith, saying, "Anyone who does not provide for their relatives, and especially for their own household, has denied the faith and is worse than an unbeliever" (1 Tim. 5:8). He gave strict rules to husbands, wives, fathers, children, and even slaves. See the comprehensive nature of his instructions:

Husbands, love your wives, just as Christ loved the church and gave himself up for her. (Eph. 5:25)

Wives, submit yourselves to your own husbands as you do to the Lord. (Eph. 5:22)

Fathers, do not exasperate your children; instead, bring them up in the training and instruction of the Lord. (Eph. 6:4)

Children, obey your parents in the Lord, for this is right. (Eph. 6:1)

Slaves, obey your earthly masters with respect and fear, and with sincerity of heart, just as you would obey Christ. (Eph. 6:5)

Group conversion of several families is recorded in the New Testament. Cornelius the Gentile and his whole household were filled with the Spirit and baptized in water in one day (Acts 10). Lydia and members of her household were baptized in the same day (Acts 16:14–15). The Philippian jailer and his family were baptized in the same night (Acts 16:33). According to the New Testament, God wants to save the families and bless them.

The early Christians did not have fancy places of worship. We are told that they met from house to house. Houses were centers of prayer and worship (Acts 12:12). House churches became the norm as synagogues became less and less available to Christians. Look at the place of homes in the Christian community following the day of Pentecost as described by Luke: "They broke bread in their homes and ate together with glad and sincere hearts, praising God and enjoying the favor of all the people. And the Lord added to their number daily those who were being saved" (Acts 2:46–47).

It appears that the community met in family homes and eventually *became* the family. Those who were losing their biological families on account of their faith were adopting the community of faith as their new family. Jesus had prepared them for this transfer of affiliation.

> Do not suppose that I have come to bring peace to the earth. I did not come to bring peace, but a sword. For I have come to turn "a man against his father, a daughter against her mother, a daughter-in-law against her mother-in-law—a man's enemies will be the members of his own household." Anyone who loves their father or mother more than me is not worthy of me; anyone who loves their son or daughter more than me is not worthy of me. . . . Anyone who welcomes you welcomes me, and anyone who welcomes me welcomes the one who sent me . . . And if anyone gives even a cup of cold water to one of these little ones who is my disciple, truly I tell you, that person will certainly not lose their reward. (Matt.10:34–42)

The church is the people of God. Church members are children of God. They are members of the household of faith. All Christians are brothers and sisters in Christ. There is no Jew or Gentile, male or female, free or slave in Christ (Col. 3:11). A radically new family has been created by God, the Creator of the original family. One is born into this family through the work of the Spirit at the new birth. Born of the Spirit, one is born again into this family of God. Jews have been members of God's household for a long time. The Gentiles were then added to this family. Jews and Gentiles are now members of the same household.

There is no one without a family now. Those without a father and mother now find them in the community of faith. Those who lost their brothers and sisters one way or another now find them in the church. Those who were rejected by their biological families are now accepted in the new family of God. Men, women, children, orphans, widows, elderly, married, singles, Jews, and Gentiles—all find a family in God's household. This is indeed radical and hard to conceive in our age of nuclear families. But this is our household.

In this family, you are eternally loved. On July 29, 1981, the most highly publicized and unbelievably glamorous wedding took place in England. The groom was Great Britain's heir apparent, Prince Charles. The bride was Lady Diana Spencer. It was reported that forty-five hundred pots of fresh flowers lined the route to St. Paul's Cathedral, where the ceremony took place, and about twenty-five hundred guests filled the sanctuary. According to some reports, twenty-one cameras run by seventy-five technicians brought the video of the ceremony to living rooms across the world. An estimated 715 million people worldwide watched it in real time. This should have been the wedding of the twentieth century, but the fairy tale turned out to be a nightmare. After separations, accusations, betrayals, and sins, the marriage broke up and the princess died.

All the money in the world and all the glamour in the universe do not guarantee true and lasting love or stable and nurturing family. All earthly love has limitations because we belong to a fallen world. True and everlasting love is found only in God and His family. The Bible tells us that God so loved the world

(John 3:16). God's love is so global and at the same time so personal. God loves us in His own unconditional way forever. God loved us so much that He gave us His only Son Jesus and through Him a new family. While we were still sinners, Christ died for us (Rom. 5:8). God loved us so much that He gave us not only Christ, but through Him, everything we need for this life and the life to come (Rom. 8:32). The community of faith as the family of God is part of this provision.

God's love is unconditional and eternal. We are loved just as we are with an eternal love. Human love is conditional, limited, and often unreliable. God's love is unconditional, unlimited, and completely reliable. Nothing in this world or the world to come shall separate us from God's love. Listen to Paul:

> Who shall separate us from the love of Christ? Shall trouble or hardship or persecution or famine or nakedness or danger or sword? As it is written: "For your sake we face death all day long; we are considered as sheep to be slaughtered." No, in all these things we are more than conquerors through him who loved us. For I am convinced that neither death nor life, neither angels nor demons, neither the present nor the future, nor any powers, neither height nor depth, nor anything else in all creation, will be able to separate us from the love of God that is in Christ Jesus our Lord. (Rom. 8:35–39)

This is wonderful news.

In this family, you are forever remembered. In God's family, all members share significance and worth, and everyone is remembered forever. Listen to the promise: "Can a mother forget the baby at her breast and have no compassion on the child she has borne? Though she may forget, I will not forget you! See, I have engraved you on the palms of my hands" (Isa. 49:15–16). God was responding to Israel when they complained that He had forgotten them. God's answer is clear: can a woman forget her nursing child? It is impossible to imagine a mother forgetting her nursing child, but even if such a thing could happen, God will not forget His children. This is guaranteed because He has engraved their names on the palms of His hands.

According to God's Word, the only thing God seems to forget is our sins. "I will forgive their wickedness and remember their sins no more" (Jer. 31:34). The record is clear that God remembers His children. God remembered Noah (Gen. 8:1), God remembered Abraham (Gen. 19:29). God remembered Rachel, and Hannah (Gen. 8:1; 19:29; 30:22; 1 Sam. 1:19). He will remember you also. His prophetic evidence: "I have engraved you on the palms of my hands" (Isa 49:16). In other words, He has inscribed us (carved us), not in the sky, not on the mountainside, or in the ocean waves, but in His own palms.

When was this? When were God's hands carved? It must be when God became man in Jesus, lived in our neighborhood, and was crucified on a cross. Remember the hands of Jesus?

* The hands that took five loaves, blessed them, broke them, and gave to the hungry multitude.
* The hands that touched blind eyes and healed them.

* The hands that touched the untouchable leper and cleansed him.
* The hands that took up little children to bless them.
* The hands that caught Peter when he was sinking.
* The hands that took bread on the night of betrayal, broke it, and gave to his disciples, saying, "This is my body" (Matt. 26:26).

One day His enemies led Him to a place called Calvary and stretched out those hands on a wooden cross and nailed them to it. Take a closer look at those hands. You may see more than wounds; you may see your own name engraved there. If you don't believe it, ask Thomas, the apostle who went to India. One day he took a look at those hands. The gospel of John tells us the story. Thomas was not there when the risen Jesus first appeared to His disciples. He had trouble believing their testimony of seeing the risen Lord and said, "Unless I see the nail marks in his hands and put my finger where the nails were, and put my hand into his side, I will not believe" (John 20:25). Jesus returned after a week and startled Thomas with these words, "Put your finger here; see my hands. Reach out your hand and put it into my side. Stop doubting and believe." Overwhelmed, Thomas could only exclaim, "My Lord and my God!" (vv. 27–28). Could it be that Thomas saw not only the wounds of Jesus, but also his own name carved in those wounds? This could happen to you.

It is clear that the resurrected body of Jesus still had wounds from the crucifixion. It appears that the mark of those wounds remain with him eternally (John 20:27). The cross was in our past, redeeming us. The cross is in our present, healing us. The cross will be in our future too. Truly, God made history by the cross of Jesus and divided it at the cross.

* Satan was defeated at the cross.
* Sin was made powerless at the cross.
* Death was destroyed at the cross.
* Evil was overcome at the cross.
* Love exploded at the cross.
* Reconciliation prevailed at the cross.
* Burdens were lifted at the cross.
* God said yes to us at the cross.
* The grave lost its victory at the cross.
* Salvation was bought at the cross.
* Condemnation was removed at the cross.
* We were forgiven at the cross.
* Sicknesses were healed at the cross.

Because of the cross, our sorrow has turned to joy, our night has turned to day, and our death has turned to life.

Now the weak can say I am strong.
The poor can say I am rich.
The blind can say I can see.

The cross is a memorial both to God and us. It reminds us of God's redemptive action on our behalf, and it keeps our names before God through the nail wounds of His Son. He will not forget us.

I am reminded of a beautiful young woman I met as a patient at the City of Faith Hospital, where I served as a chaplain. She was a born-again Christian who had no family members to visit her. Her mother and grandmother had died from breast cancer, her father was also dead, and she had no siblings. She lived alone and kept her sickness a secret without seeking medical help as long as she could, due to fear. According to the doctors, the prognosis was not good because by the time she came to the hospital, the disease had progressed significantly.

One day she asked me during a pastoral visit, "I have no family left. I don't know how long I will live. Can I ask you for a favor?"

Thinking that she would ask for some practical help, I said, "Of course. What can I do for you?"

She asked, "Would you remember me once I am gone?"

Moved by her unexpected request, I said, "Certainly. I will remember you." That was our last visit.

We all want to be remembered. The Bible assures us that God remembers us as His children and as members of His household. He will never forget us for we have been carved in his hands, engraved forever. As members of His family, we will be remembered forever.

I was privileged to be raised in a pastor's home in India. I have encountered many hardships due to my place of birth and circumstances, but was fortunate to receive much affirmation and love both from my biological family and from the church families my father pastored. My wife had a background similar to mine. We have tried to offer a safe and loving home for our two daughters, who are adults now. But I recognize that this is not the case with many of our friends and readers.

I don't know what kind of biological family you came from. I don't know if you were the star of your family of origin or the opposite. It does not matter anymore. Praise God if your earthly family is healthy and loving, but do not despair if not. You now belong to the most loving family on earth. You are a beloved child in that family, and a star forever and ever (Dan. 12:3). You are special!

Questions for Reflection

1. Compare and contrast the concept of family in the Bible with that in our current culture.
2. What is your understanding of God as a father and mother?
3. Support the idea that God works in and through families.
4. What do we learn from the New Testament genealogies of Jesus?
5. How did Jesus show concern for family?
6. Discuss the salvation of three households in the book of Acts and the role of the homes in the life of the early church.
7. What were Paul's essential instructions regarding family?
8. Discuss the idea that the church (the community of faith) is the new family of God.
9. Discuss the characteristics and benefits of the Christian community as a family.
10. Review your experience as a member of your biological family and the church family and consider any lessons.

Chapter 3

▲ ▲ ▲

You Are a Disciple of Jesus Christ

"Therefore go and make disciples of all
nations, baptizing them in the name of the
Father and of the Son and of the Holy Spirit,
and teaching them to obey everything I have
commanded you. And surely I am with
you always, to the very end of the age."

—MATTHEW 28:19–20

There is a crisis brewing in the American church. It has to do with the main business of the church, which is making disciples. Underneath several major concerns within the church and within evangelical Christianity in particular is this issue of missing discipleship. Even churches that claim an increase in their membership cannot boast about an increase in discipleship.

Unfortunately, most of the mainline churches are declining in membership and social impact.

Pastors I have spoken to agree with this diagnosis, but there is no evidence that this concern is translating into significant and widely implemented remedial actions. We have programs to help people with all sorts of problems, but not enough to guide them on their development as disciples of Jesus Christ. We are failing to move people from membership to discipleship.

We live in a country where, according to Gallup, 77 percent of the population claim to be Christian.[6] Forty-four percent claim to belong to a local congregation, according to a US religion census (2010), but only about half of them actually show up to worship weekly. This is not a glowing testimony.

According to Christian missiologist and researcher Ed Stetzer,[7] there are three types of professing Christians: *Cultural Christians*, *Congregational Christians*, and *Committed Christians*. Each congregation seems to have a general constituency or parish, a worshipping congregation, and a group of committed Christians, in decreasing order of size.

Cultural Christianity in Stetzer's view is closer to deism than to Christian faith. It affirms the faith without living it and believes the dogma without practicing it. Congregational Christianity is not much better, as it allows one to belong to

---

6 Frank Newport, "In U.S., 77% Identify as Christian," Gallup, December 24, 2012, http://www.gallup.com/poll/159548/identify-christian.aspx.

7 Ed Stetzer, "Is the Church Dying in the U.S.? Redefining Christians as Cultural, Congregational, & Convictional," Vision Room, accessed March 4, 2017, http://visionroom.com/church-dying-u-s-redefining-christians-cultural-congregational-convictional/.

a community without necessarily supporting it, making one a spectator rather than a participant. True discipleship of committed Christians has to be intentional, according to Stetzer, engaging the Bible, involving small groups, and focusing on spiritual growth.

Many seem to be happy to have church membership rather than Christian discipleship. They prefer to be fans of Jesus rather than friends. The lack of discipleship among Christians has a significant impact on the nation, particularly in business, education, and politics. Civil religion and cultural Christianity cannot transform a community or nation. Religion manipulated by clever politicians for their own purposes cannot impact the world for God or influence communities with the principles of the kingdom of God. A culture of life and concern for ethics stem from true Christianity and are nurtured by costly discipleship. Cultural Christians conveniently claiming Judeo-Christian heritage cannot transform the nation. They can only create a form of godliness without the power thereof (2 Tim. 3:5). It takes men and women who have counted the cost of discipleship to impact the world with God's healing.

Churches must go back to Christ's mandate: "Go and make disciples of all nations, baptizing them in the name of the Father and of the Son and of the Holy Spirit, and teaching them to obey everything I have commanded you" (Matt. 28:19–20). God's will is that Christ be formed in us. Paul the apostle considered this extremely painful to accomplish. He expressed this sentiment to the Galatian believers: "My dear children, . . . I am again in the pains of childbirth until Christ is formed in you" (Gal. 4:19).

I recall my daughter and her husband looking anxiously at an ultrasound film to see the image of their first son for the first time several months before he was born. I can imagine God looking intensely into our souls to see if the image of His Son is being formed in us. The purpose of discipleship is spiritual formation, which is measured in terms of Christlikeness in the believer. "For those God foreknew he conformed to the likeness of his Son, that he might be the firstborn among many brothers and sisters" (Rom. 8:29).

LeRoy Eims, the well-known author on discipleship, was right: a church that does not produce disciples is like a shoe factory that is running around the clock but not producing any shoes![8] We have too many of these in this nation.

Discipleship has to do with our relationship with Christ. It boils down to our proximity to Him or distance from Him. We can evaluate our relationship with the Lord in terms of biblical images. For instance, we can ask ourselves the following questions:

* Would I have belonged with the 5,000 who enjoyed the bread and fish, or the 120 who waited in the upper room?
* Would I have been among the 70 who were sent out to evangelize, or the 12 called to follow Jesus closely?

---

8 Leroy Eims, *The Lost Art of Disciple Making* (Grand Rapids, MI: Zondervan, 1978), 59 – 61.

* Would I have been one of the three—Peter, James, and John—who accompanied Jesus to the Mount of Transfiguration?
* Am I more like John, who stood alone by the cross on the dreadful Friday, or like the one who gave him up for a bag of coins?

These are sobering thoughts.

A disciple lives under the lordship of Jesus. Jesus is not just a disciple's Savior or healer. He becomes the Lord of that individual's life. A disciple lives under the authority of Jesus, acknowledging that He holds all authority. The gospel of Luke testifies to the authority of Jesus in all area of human life. Chapter 8 gives a synopsis of this truth by illustrating Jesus' authority over (1) natural forces (vv. 22–25), (2) demonic power (vv. 26–39), (3) sickness (vv. 42b–48), and (4) death (vv. 40–42a, 49–56):

Jesus Has Authority over Natural Forces. While Jesus and the disciples were sailing across the Sea of Galilee, Jesus fell asleep. A great storm arose, which put them in grave danger, so the disciples cried out to Jesus and woke Him up. He rebuked the wind and the waves, and they obeyed Him. Luke testifies of Jesus' authority over natural forces, which included stormy seas!

Jesus Has Authority over Demonic Power. Luke went on to report the healing of a demon-possessed man in the region of the Gadarenes. This man was living in the tombs, naked and deranged, but when he met Jesus, he fell at His feet. "Jesus asked him, 'What is your name?' 'Legion,' he replied, because many demons had gone into him. And they begged him repeatedly not to order them to go into the Abyss" (Luke 8:30–31). Jesus gave the demons permission to go into a herd of nearby pigs. The herd rushed into the lake and drowned, but the man who was set free sat at the feet of Jesus, "dressed and in his right mind" (v. 35). According to Luke, Jesus has authority over demonic forces. They tremble at His presence and obey Him.

Jesus Has Authority over Sickness. Luke reports that upon Jesus' return from the region of the Gadarenes, a great crowd greeted Him and almost crushed Him. A particular woman in that crowd had been suffering from chronic bleeding for twelve years. Physicians could not heal her, and she was desperate. As this nameless woman came up behind Jesus and touched the edge of His garment, she was instantly healed. "Who touched me?" Jesus asked. "Someone touched me; I know that power has gone out of me," He added (vv. 45, 46). The woman came forward, fell at His feet, and gave her testimony. "Daughter, your faith has healed you. Go in peace" (v. 48). In this passage, Luke shows that Jesus has authority over sicknesses and even over incurable diseases.

Jesus Has Authority over Death. Luke 8 ends with the story of Jesus raising the daughter of a man named Jairus, a synagogue ruler. While Jesus was ministering to the woman He had just healed, word came to Jairus that his beloved daughter was dead. Jesus said to Jairus, "Don't be afraid; just believe, and she will be healed" (v. 50). Jesus accompanied Jairus to his house and raised the twelve-year-old girl from the dead. "Her spirit returned, and at once she stood up" (v. 55). In this account,

Luke presents the evidence for Jesus' ultimate authority, which extends even over the last enemy, death.

Matthew concluded his gospel with the words of Jesus: "All authority in heaven and on earth has been given to me. Therefore go and make disciples of all nations, baptizing them in the name of the Father and of the Son and of the Holy Spirit, and teaching them to obey everything I have commanded you. And surely I am with you always, to the very end of the age" (Matt. 28:18–20). Jesus has all authority and He has given it to His disciples, who are called to represent Him and His kingdom in this world. A true disciple accepts Jesus' authority over his own life and ministers to others in the authority given to him by Jesus. Discipleship involves both living under authority and exercising appropriate authority.

We must remember that until we were called Christians for the first time in Antioch, we were called disciples. Disciples are followers and learners (see Luke 6:40 KJV). We follow Jesus and learn from Him. We learn character (Gal. 5:22–23), convictions (Heb. 11:24–25), skills (Mark 7:37), and perspective (Rom. 12:1–2) from Christ and His Word. We are apprentices who imitate the master and gain skills. Christ has called us (Matt. 4:19) and we have responded. There is no turning back (Luke 9:62).

As disciples, we abide in Jesus the vine and bear fruit (John 15:5–8). We love Christ and are willing to deny ourselves and carry the cross (Luke 14:26, 11; 9:23; 14:27). We love others and are committed to serving them in the name of Christ (John 13:34–35; Matt. 10:25; 25:40).

Discipleship is a formational journey and it is transformational in effect. God's grace not only accepts and saves us, but it also transforms us. Discipleship moves people from decision (for Christ) to true conversion, and from conversion to sanctification. Disciples of Christ take the apostle's exhortation seriously: "Do not conform to the pattern of this world, but be transformed by the renewing of your mind. Then you will be able to test and approve what God's will is—his good, pleasing and perfect will" (Rom. 12:2).

True formation happens within a community, and it involves one's body, mind, spirit, and relationships. Paul summarized this process: "May God himself, the God of peace, sanctify you through and through. May your whole spirit, soul and body be kept blameless at the coming of our Lord Jesus Christ" (1 Thess. 5:23). The Word of God, the Spirit of Christ, and the community of faith are involved in this journey of faith.

Discipleship is a growth process. Some have studied it in stages. While there are several models of spiritual growth, my favorite one was developed by Professor Chuck Farah at Oral Roberts University, who was a mentor and a colleague to me. He called his model "types" of faith. According to Farah, the lowest level of discipleship is called *historical faith*. This is faith based on other individuals or one's church affiliation. In this stage, one sees oneself as a part of a denomination or a heritage. Faith is not personally owned; it is corporate in nature with minimum personal commitment.

Farah called the next level *temporary faith*. This is a stage in which one's faith is activated, but remains so only for a short period. Like the seeds that fell among thorns in Jesus' parable (Matt. 13:1–23), the spiritual awakening is temporary.

The next type is called *saving faith*. Here one experiences new birth in Christ. Unfortunately, many are stuck at this stage for a long time. They can claim to be Christians, but there is no spiritual growth taking place. Many people at the congregational level of Christian life are at this stage.

Farah calls the next level *faith for miracles*. One is open to the work of the Spirit in this stage, but faith here is something one has to "work up." It is not something that flows easily through one's life. This is where one's faith is built on rules, regulations, and formulas.

The next level is called *gift faith*. Here one is growing in God and is allowing the gifts of the Spirit to manifest in and through one's life. Faith is not something worked up in this level; it is truly a gift received from God. There are people who reach the level of gift faith, but they do not have the character to match the gifts. They often self-sabotage due to a lack of discipline in their lives.

Farah called the next level of faith *fruit faith*. This denotes active discipleship and testifies to significant spiritual growth. True discipleship changes one's character. The gifts of the Spirit are given, but the fruits of the Spirit are cultivated. This cultivation happens only through a process and must involve others. No one reaches this stage in isolation and solo practice. This is where the church can improve by providing more intentional opportunities for potential disciples to grow.

The highest level of discipleship involves the type of faith Farah called *ministry faith*. This is when one is able to minister to others instead of being preoccupied with one's own needs. A mature disciple is able to share the gospel with others and nurture them. In some other models of discipleship, this stage is called *workers*, *leaders*, and so on. I prefer Farah's model because it focuses on ministry without confining it to working or leading. One realizes at this stage that faith is not just for receiving something from God; rather it is for giving something to others. This highest level of faith is about giving, not receiving; it is about ministering to others, not expecting ministry from others. We must disciple and mentor Christians, especially new believers, to reach their full potential as followers of Jesus.

A young evangelist I met in India a few years ago is an example of the possibilities of true discipleship. I met him at the conclusion of my father's funeral service. My father was the pastor of a South Indian congregation for three decades while he served as a district supervisor in his denomination. The young minister wanted to express his gratitude for my father's ministry in that part of the world, and particularly the impact he'd had on his personal life. He said, "When I first met your father, I met him as his shoe repairman. He became a spiritual father and mentor to me. Today I serve as a minister because of his investment in my life." Somehow, my father, without the benefit of an Ivy League education, as I had, turned his shoe repairman into a preacher of the gospel through discipleship and mentoring. I am still trying to figure out how to do it, but I am convinced that it is indeed possible.

The ultimate purpose of discipleship is to produce transformed individuals who can minister. Here ministry is not limited to ordained vocation or full-time Christian service. It is defined as being an active disciple of Jesus Christ; it is about living as whole persons in a broken world. In other words, it is about living the lifestyle of the kingdom of God.

I found a way for a Christian to self-monitor to see how he or she is growing and developing as a disciple. This is based on what Paul Pruyser in his book *The Minister as a Diagnostician* calls *pastoral diagnostic themes*. These themes, normally used by pastoral counselors to make spiritual diagnoses, allow us to examine our own discipleship.

Pruyser's themes provide us several practical dimensions to assess with regard to our health and well-being as disciples of Jesus Christ.[9]

1) Our *awareness of the holy*. A healthy Christian must be aware of the presence of a holy God in his or her life. People often describe their life issues in such a way that one wonders where God is in respect to their situation. An individual's awareness of the presence of God in his or her life is a sign of healthy discipleship.

2) Our *sense of Providence*. Providence is a theological term that means that God the Creator takes care of His creation. Healthy disciples are those who have an assurance

---

9 The following is adapted from Paul W. Pruyser, *The Minister as Diagnostician: Personal Problems in Pastoral Perspective* (Philadelphia: Westminster John Knox Press, 1976), 61–79.

that God will meet their needs so that they can face the challenges and issues of life from a position of confidence. God's providence covers His entire creation. A sense of providence enables an individual to live by faith, in the knowledge that God will supply all his or her needs through Christ Jesus (Phil. 4:19).

3) Our *faith*. A growing person is one who looks at his or her world through the eyes of faith. Just as eyeglasses affect a person's vision, faith affects one's view of life. A healthy disciple walks by faith and not by sight alone. Faith enables an individual to believe in God's providence; faith believes that God is faithful. When we consider all the "by faith" statements in Hebrews 11, it becomes clear that the author was describing life as an adventure of faith. A healthy disciple has this type of faith.

4) Our *gratefulness*. A healthy disciple lives a thankful life in which his or her attitude is based on gratitude. Unfortunately, gratefulness is a rare commodity in an affluent society. A healthy disciple enjoys God's grace with gratitude. Gratitude does not depend on the size of the gift; it flows out of one's relationship with the giver.

5) Our *process of repenting*. All born-again Christians believe that God has forgiven their sins. The Christian life is a forgiven life. All of us, however, are subject to sins of commission and omission. This means that we must live with an attitude of repentance. The ability to experience *metanoia* (repentance), to ask for

forgiveness, and to live in humility is evidence of a spiritually wholesome life.

6) Our *feeling of communion*. The Bible speaks about the fellowship of the saints; a sense of community fosters fellowship. A growing disciple experiences communion with God and with the members of the community of faith. This extends beyond the sacrament of communion, to a sense of belonging and intimacy within the local community of faith and the extended family of God. A healthy disciple has the capacity for intimacy with both God and humanity. All of us have met long-term members of a particular church who describe the church as "their" church. Regardless of the cause, this attitude reflects the absence of a sense of communion with the body of Christ. Having a sense of belonging and community is a sign of spiritual growth and development.

7) Our *sense of vocation*. In Christian life, all are called by God; therefore, all Christians must see their lifework, whatever that might be, as a vocation. In this perspective, both "professional" ministry and "secular" employment become God-given vocations. We are called to do all as unto Christ (Eph. 6:5; Col. 3:17). A healthy disciple is one who sees his or her life's calling as a God-given vocation.

Pruyser's themes are important clues to true discipleship. We will benefit from examining our lives with respect to these themes, as they are indicators of our growth and development as disciples of Jesus Christ. After all, as disciples we are called "to grow in the grace and knowledge of our Lord and Savior Jesus Christ" (2 Peter 3:18).

Discipleship has to do with spiritual formation, which does not happen without the work of the Holy Spirit. A true disciple allows the Holy Spirit to work in and through him or her. The book of Acts testifies that the Spirit did four specific things in the earliest disciples' lives:

* He empowered them.
* He extended their vision.
* He enabled them to embrace strangers.
* He transformed them.

The Spirit empowers. The Holy Spirit is the source of power to witness beyond our abilities. The disciples who waited in the upper room and received the Holy Spirit on the day of Pentecost were empowered by the Spirit. The Holy Spirit became the power for these early Christians to witness beyond their abilities. A new boldness possessed this petrified group (Acts 4:20; 5:29; 7:54–60; 9:31) as a result of receiving the Holy Spirit. Signs and wonders took place beyond the ministries of the leaders, through the work of others in near and far places (8:8). The Spirit began to move in places such as Antioch through ordinary people who were not apostles who were the presumed administrators of the divine work.

The Holy Spirit extends vision. When the Spirit came, Christian faith moved from being local to being global; the disciples experienced an expansion of their vision. It seems that things Jesus had told them began to make more sense to them after they were filled with the Spirit. They watched the 120 people in the upper room becoming 3,000 believers in one day. The community grew and its vision and mission expanded. The whole world was in Jerusalem on the day of Pentecost, and Jerusalem was about to go to the whole world. The church was adding members at the beginning, but soon it seemed to be multiplying membership.

The Holy Spirit impacted the early disciples' worldview. They had once been local people with limited vision. Pentecost extended their vision and launched them out to people in faraway places they had not considered before.

The Holy Spirit enables disciples to embrace strangers. The Spirit brought strangers into the church, and the church was able to embrace them. This was not always the case with the disciples. The Spirit began to remove internal and external hindrances within people and in the community to grow the church. Distance was no longer a barrier. Samaria and Antioch were reached. Gender was not an obstacle. Women were included in the life and ministry of the community. Both sons and daughters were teaching and prophesying, finally (Acts 18:26; 21:9). Titles were not a barrier to relationships and ministry. Deacons, not just apostles, were ministering signs and wonders. Race was not an issue anymore. The 120 in the upper room in

Acts 2 were basically a Jewish group. In Acts 3, a handicapped person came in. In chapter 6, Greek women were being taken care of. Samaritans were coming into the fold in chapter 8. The Ethiopian, an African, was included in chapter 8. The Gentile Cornelius was welcomed in chapter 10. Lydia, the European businesswoman, was included in chapter 16. The Spirit enabled the local group to embrace the world and demonstrate global diversity!

The Holy Spirit transforms. The Holy Spirit transformed individuals and communities in the first-century church. Communities were transformed in Jerusalem and Ephesus as people touched by the Spirit were personally transformed. Peter's life is an excellent case study. He was the disciple who had said no to several key initiatives. He had said no to crucifixion (Matt. 16:21–23). He was on record opposing Jesus washing his feet (John 13:8). He definitely said no to the idea of going to the house of a Gentile such as Cornelius (see Acts 10, esp. vv. 14, 28). He was, however, persuaded by unbelievable divine appointments to go and visit Cornelius. He preached Jesus at the house of this Gentile, and the results completely surprised him and everyone else involved. "While Peter was still speaking . . . the Holy Spirit came on all who heard the message. The circumcised believers who had come with Peter were astonished that the gift of the Holy Spirit had been poured out even on Gentiles. For they heard them speaking in tongues and praising God. Then Peter said, 'Surely no one can stand in the way of their being baptized with water. They have received the Holy Spirit just as we have'" (10:44–47).

Peter was transformed by the Holy Spirit's work in him. He was never the same again. His transformation was significant and strategic for the purposes of God. Later, this very apostle, who was once adamant about Jewish prerequisites for Christian initiation, defended the opposite position on diversity at the Jerusalem conference (Acts 15:6–10). Amazing, indeed! He was transformed by the Spirit. A disciple is a person transformed by the power of the Holy Spirit.

You are a disciple of Jesus Christ. You live under His authority and you minister to others in the authority given to you by Him. You have been sanctified by God's Word and the blood of Jesus, and transformed by the power of His Spirit. Grow in the grace and knowledge of our Lord and Savior. Claim your identity and authority as a disciple of Jesus Christ, and walk in the power of your transformed life.

Questions for Reflection

1. What are your thoughts on the need of discipleship in the church today?
2. Comment on the idea of having three groups of Christians in the world and in each congregation.
3. What is your definition of a disciple of Jesus Christ?
4. List the major characteristics of a disciple.
5. What does this chapter teach about the authority of Jesus and the authority of the disciple?
6. Identify the seven types of faith according to Professor Chuck Farah.
7. What are the indicators of spiritual growth based on Paul Pruyser's diagnostic themes?
8. What are the four outcomes of the work of the Holy Spirit in the early disciples, as seen in the book of Acts?
9. What are your thoughts on the role of community in the process of spiritual formation and transformation?
10. What area of your life is experiencing the transforming presence of the Holy Spirit?

Chapter 4

You Are a Citizen of the Kingdom of God

But our citizenship is in heaven. And we eagerly await a Savior from there, the Lord Jesus Christ.

—PHILIPPIANS 3:20

Several reliable surveys show that there is not much difference between the lifestyles of Americans who claim to be Christians and those who do not. Researcher George Barna has reported that only 9 percent of born-again adults have a biblical worldview.[10] Another 6 percent have what may be called a biblical foundation for living, which means 85 percent of all

---

10 Ed Stetzer, "Barna: How Many Have a Biblical Worldview?" *CT*, March 9, 2009, n.p., http://www.christianitytoday.com/edstetzer/2009/march/barna-how-many-have-biblical-worldview.html.

born-again adults have neither the basic Christian foundation nor a biblical worldview. According to Barna, most born-again Christians base their moral choices on their feelings, not the Word of God![11]

There are many ways to process this information. This is my take: modern Christians lack a true understanding of the concept of the kingdom of God that Jesus taught, the lifestyle it requires, and the invitation they received to embody it.

Preaching the kingdom of God is not a safe occupation. John the Baptist came preaching the kingdom of God, and he was beheaded. Jesus picked up the message, saying, "Repent, for the kingdom of God is at hand" (Mark 1:15, paraphrased), and He was crucified. His disciples continued the message, and they also had to pay with their lives.

God always finds individuals who will declare the arrival of His kingdom, and that declaration begins with a call to repentance. The world does not like such a call, but kingdom life begins with repentance. In the Gospels, "repent" is not a request; it is a command. Jesus told Zacchaeus, "Come down!" and to Matthew He said, "Follow me." To the rich young ruler, Jesus said, "Sell your possessions and give to the poor" (Luke 19:5; Matt. 9:9; 19:21). These were not meant as requests; they were commands.

We are all familiar with the idea of naturalization, the process through which an immigrant becomes a citizen. Unfortunately, no one is naturalized into the kingdom of God; one must be "born again" (John 3:3, 7). Two kingdoms exist—the kingdom

---

11 Stetzer, n.p.

of darkness and the kingdom of light—and you must die in one to enter the other. More specifically, you must die in one to be born into the other. The kingdom of God is a kingdom of light and life. As we enter the kingdom of life, we pass from death to life.

The kingdom of God is a divine concept. It is not meat or drink; it has to do with righteousness, peace, and joy in the Holy Spirit (Rom. 14:17). It actually means the rule and reign of God.

We may say that there are four dimensions of the kingdom of God that will inform us about adopting a kingdom lifestyle on planet Earth:

* the concept of time in the kingdom of God
* the values of the kingdom of God
* the priorities of the kingdom of God
* the mysteries of the kingdom of God

Let's look at these one by one.

The concept of time in the kingdom of God. According to the Word of God, the kingdom of God has arrived; it arrived when Jesus came into the world and announced, "The kingdom of God is at hand." The kingdom of God involves the past, present, and the future. In terms of the past, the kingdom has come (Matt. 3:2; 12:28). Concerning the present, the kingdom of God is here now; it is in our midst, manifesting the power of the Holy Spirit (Luke 17:21). With respect to the future, the kingdom of God is yet coming (Matt. 6:10). The cosmic fullness of the kingdom of God is yet to come.

So we live now between the kingdom come and the kingdom coming. We live by faith now and enjoy many benefits of the kingdom of God. Salvation, healing, signs and wonders, and the gifts of the Spirit are current benefits of the kingdom of God. And yet, there is a level of kingdom fullness we have not seen so far. Not all our prayers are answered now. Not all suffering is removed yet. The innocent still suffer. The sick are not all healed. Loved ones die. Persecution does go on. But the fullness of God's kingdom will come. Until then, knowing that the suffering of this present time is not worthy to be compared with the glory that will be revealed in us (Rom. 8:18), we continue to pray, "Father, thy kingdom come!" We know that when that day comes, God will wipe away all our tears (Isa. 25:8).

So how shall we live between the kingdom come and the kingdom coming? The answer is simple: we shall live by faith in the Son of God, who loved us and gave Himself for us (Eph. 5:2). We will live a kingdom lifestyle in this world. What does the kingdom lifestyle look like? Before we can answer that, we must consider the values, priorities, and mysteries of the kingdom of God.

The values of the kingdom of God. The values of God's kingdom are upside down. For instance, in God's kingdom, giving is the way to receiving: "Give, and it will be given to you. A good measure, pressed down, shaken together and running over, will be poured into your lap. For with the measure you use, it will be measured to you" (Luke 6:38). In the kingdom of God, serving is the way to lead because the last shall be first (Mark 10:31), and dying is the way to live: "Whoever wants to be my disciple must deny themselves and take up their cross and follow me. For whoever wants to save their life will lose it, but whoever loses their life for me and for the gospel will save it" (Mark 8:34–35).

These are not just abstract theoretical positions for a citizen of the kingdom of God. These are actual values we are expected to live by. There is no way to live this way without a cost. I have seen many young people and new believers shocked to find out that they lost friends or jobs because of the kingdom values they adopted. I know people who were denied professional advancement because they refused to compromise their kingdom convictions. Some faced discrimination. Others faced ridicule. I remember my parents and grandparents in India taking in newly converted Christians into their homes who were disowned by their loved ones and disinherited by their families because they responded to the Lord's invitation to join His kingdom. Yes, there is a price to pay, but I have also seen the Lord opening wider doors and incredible opportunities to many who remained faithful.

The priorities of the kingdom of God. The priorities of God's kingdom are also unlike the world's. In the kingdom, formation is more important than information, and unconditional love is paramount. The kingdom is governed by the principles of *agape* (unconditional love). This love goes beyond neighborly or brotherly love; it is more like trinity love. What does trinity love look like? According to Juan Carlos Ortiz, author of the well-known book *Disciple*,[12] it looks like mashed potatoes. You can

---

12 Juan Carlos Ortiz, *Disciple* (Carol Stream: Creation House, 1975), 60–64.

claim unity just by being together with others, like potatoes in a sack. They can sing about unity, saying, "We are in the same bag, and we have the same brand name." But they could also say, "I am a big potato and you are a small potato;" or, "Look at me; I'm a white potato; you are a brown potato." Often, this is the only kind of unity that we have in our churches. But if you take the potatoes out of the bag, peel them, cut them into pieces, put them in a pot, boil them, and make mashed potatoes, something new happens to these potatoes. They are the same potatoes, but now no one can distinguish the big potato from the small potato. One cannot tell the difference between the white potato and the brown one because they have become one. This kind of love represents trinity love, which allows us to sing, "We are one in the Spirit; we are one in the Lord."[13] The authentic Christian life is a life that gives priority to love and unity.

Most of us are not used to agape love, because it is unconditional and divine in nature. We have become accustomed to conditional love, which I call "if" or "because of" love. God presents us with "in spite of" love, and He desires that we be filled with this love. Several years ago, I met a woman who told me that she had learned how to prevent cancer. She gave me her secret: drink as much carrot juice as you can, three times a day. She has been practicing this strategy for many years, and I believe it works. She is healthy, and she has no cancer, but she has one slight problem: She now looks like a carrot! It appears that if you fill yourself with carrot juice long enough, your skin will reflect the color of carrot;

---

13 "We Are One in the Spirit," copyright 1966 by Peter Scholte; see lyrics at http://www.untiedmusic.com/ezekiel/onespirt.html.

similarly, if you fill yourself with the love of God long enough, you will begin to look like the love of God.

Genuine relationships are a priority in the kingdom of God. Kingdom relationships function like the various parts of the human body; all are members of one body, uniting each other, supporting one another, passing along nourishment to one another, and making room for one another. In the kingdom, we are not in competition with one another, and we don't attack each other. We support and nurture one another.

Look at the spiritual metaphors for the church: body of Christ, building made with living stones, household of faith, family of God, and communion of saints (1 Cor. 12:27; 1 Peter 2:5; Gal 2:10; 1 Thess. 4:10; Apostle's Creed). All indicate intimate relationships. All imply strong connections and purposeful unity.

Worship is also a priority in the kingdom of God. Worship may be called the language of God's kingdom. So is preaching. Kingdom citizens are called to bear witness to the King. They are to preach that He is Savior, Healer, Lord, and King.

The mysteries of the kingdom of God. According to the parable of Jesus, the kingdom of God involves certain mysteries. First, everything about the kingdom is not visible to the eye. It is like salt in a prepared meal, not visible, but very much influential and discernible. Jesus said, "You are the salt of the earth. But if the salt loses its saltiness, how can it be made salty again? It is no longer good for anything, except to be thrown out and trampled underfoot" (Matt. 5:13). The kingdom of God is like invisible yeast that causes the dough to rise and expand. "It is like yeast that a woman took and mixed into about sixty pounds of flour until it worked all through the dough" (Luke 13:21).

Good and bad coexist in the present kingdom of God. The wheat and the tares grow together for a season, but a separation will come (Matt. 13:24–29 KJV). Good fish and bad fish will coexist in the net for a while, but a sorting will come (Matt. 13:47–49). This is a mystery.

Another mystery is that the beauty of the kingdom of God is not visible on the outside. It does not appear attractive to everyone. Like the tabernacle in the wilderness, which hosted the presence of God, the outside of the kingdom of God is unattractive. But there are those who will discover the beauty and value of the kingdom and belong to it at any cost. Like a man who finds unexpected treasure in a land and sells everything he has to buy it or a merchant who finds a pearl of great price and sells everything he has to own it, there are those who will give up everything for God's kingdom (Matt. 13:44–46). While his neighbors see only dirt, the man who gives up everything knows it contains a great treasure. The merchant is the only one recognizing the value of the pearl while others are surprised by the transaction. The kingdom of God is a mystery. What is the treasure in God's kingdom? What is the pearl of great price? In the final analysis, the treasure is Jesus. He is the pearl of great price. The one who finds Him finds everything for life now—and for eternal life. This is a great mystery.

So what is kingdom lifestyle? It means you live in a different time frame. Of course you live your life on everyday calendar time (*chronos* in Greek), but as you do, you are attuned to God's fullness of time (*kairos*). You live here and now, but your frame of reference is something beyond here and now. You accept Jesus Christ not just as your Savior and Healer, but as your Lord and Master. You live as if you have traded everything for Him. That means spiritually you have traded your degrees, homes, cars, spouse, kids, money, friends, and all else for Him. You may still formally possess all these, but they are no longer yours in your spirit or attitude. They belong to Jesus.

As a requirement of this lifestyle, you adopt kingdom values. You begin to give as if it is the very act of receiving. You die daily having been beckoned to come and die with Jesus, as Dietrich Bonhoeffer said.[14] You serve others as if your life depends on it, adopting a lifestyle of servant leadership.

Your priorities also change. You seek the kingdom of God first, knowing that everything you need will be given to you (Matt. 6:33). You live a life of repentance, loving others, worshipping God, and bearing witness to the king of glory.

You depend on God to live out the mystery of the kingdom of God in your time and place. You will preach, teach, and minister healing as the Lord gives you opportunities. You will put your hands to the plow as Jesus said and will not look back (Luke 9:62). Your lips will carry the words of the old hymn, "I have decided to follow Jesus; no turning back."[15]

I cannot end this chapter without mentioning how rewarding living the kingdom lifestyle is. The parable of the laborers in the

---

14   Dietrich Bonhoeffer, *The Cost of Discipleship*, repr. (n.p.: Touchstone, 1995), 89.

15   "I Have Decided to Follow Jesus," attr. to S. Sundar Singh, public domain. Lyrics available at http://library.timelesstruths.org/music/I_Have_Decided_to_Follow_Jesus/, accessed March 6, 2017.

vineyard gives us a glimpse of this (Matt. 20:1–15). Some came to work early in the morning; others came at the third hour, the sixth hour, and the eleventh hour. The master told them he would pay them whatever was right. When evening came, each worker received the same pay, regardless of his starting time, and those who came earlier began to complain. The master responded:

> "Friend, I am not being unfair to you. Didn't you agree to work for a denarius? Take your pay and go. I want to give the man who was hired last the same as I gave you. Don't I have the right to do what I want with my own money? Or are you envious because I am generous?" (Matt. 20:13–15)

Scholars have struggled to understand this passage, because from a contemporary perspective the pay scale seems unfair, but not if one considers that Jesus Himself is the pay. If Jesus is the ultimate currency, no greater compensation could be given to any worker in God's kingdom. In other words, those who have Jesus have everything they need for this life and the next. "He who did not spare his own Son, but gave him up for us all—how will he not also, along with him, graciously give us all things?" (Rom. 8:32).

You are a citizen of the kingdom of God. Endeavor to live the lifestyle of the kingdom of God. Internalize this identity and watch your world change dramatically.

Questions for Reflection

1. How would you define the kingdom of God?
2. Describe the concept of time in relation to the kingdom of God.
3. Present some examples of kingdom values.
4. Give some examples of kingdom priorities.
5. Comment on the mysteries of the kingdom of God.
6. What are some of the challenges facing kingdom citizens today?
7. Comment on the parables of the merchant who found great treasure.
8. Comment on the parable of the pearl of great price.
9. What aspect of the kingdom of God is most challenging to you?
10. What is the Lord saying to you about your kingdom citizenship?

Chapter 5

You Are a Whole Person, by Faith

May God himself, the God of peace, sanctify
you through and through. May your whole
spirit, soul and body be kept blameless at
the coming of our Lord Jesus Christ.

—1 Thessalonians 5:23

Among the many stories I have heard about the early days of Oral Roberts University, one regarding president Oral Roberts stands out to me. A student who had violated the university's honor code was brought before the highest discipline committee, chaired by the president, as the last step of the disciplinary process. This committee's decision would be final in all cases. The student was already suspended from the university, and he sat in the meeting, petrified about the possibility of expulsion. Instead of expelling the student, however, the committee decided to readmit him by imposing a hefty fine to be paid in cash to reenroll in his courses. Feeling dejected and having no way to make the cash payment, the student left the room, went down the stairs, and sat silently, with his head down. He was startled a few minutes later by a hand that touched his shoulder and proceeded to deposit something in his pocket. He was completely surprised to notice Oral Roberts walking away without saying anything, and even more shocked to notice that the cash he found in his pocket would help him pay the fine and return to classes. Deeply moved by the experience, the student was never the same again; he became a model student. An encounter with a person of grace and mercy can impact us greatly. Imagine having an encounter with the living God!

An encounter with the living God is a life-transforming experience. Abraham, Moses, and Joshua would testify that their individual encounters with God unnerved them and changed them. Prophets Samuel, Elijah, Isaiah, and Ezekiel would join this testimony. Young Samuel would end up replacing Eli after his encounter with God's voice (1 Sam. 3:4–11). Elijah had to run for his life after the word of the Lord came to him (1 Kings 17:2–3). Isaiah had the frightening vision of the glory of God after he saw the Lord high and lifted up in the temple (Isa. 6:1–9). Ezekiel saw dead bones becoming a living army as he encountered the voice of God (Eze. 37:1–14). All these men changed drastically as a result of their encounters.

An encounter with Jesus of Nazareth was also a life-transforming experience. There was always noticeable evidence when someone had met Jesus. The Samaritan woman who met Him wound up leaving her water pot behind and running downtown to tell everyone about the Messiah she had met (John 4:28–29). The maniac who met Jesus at a cemetery in the land of the Gadarenes soon sat at Jesus' feet, in his right mind and fully clothed! Amazingly, he later became a missionary (Luke 8:35, 38–39). The tax collector Zacchaeus who encountered Jesus and hosted him at his house started returning extorted money and giving to charity (Luke 19:8). A lame beggar was found walking and leaping and praising God after his encounter with Jesus through the ministry of the apostle Peter and friends (Acts 3:8). An Ethiopian eunuch who met Jesus through the ministry of Philip volunteered to be baptized in the desert and went on his way rejoicing (Acts 8:38). The Philippian jailer who abruptly had an introduction to Jesus following a suicide attempt was soon washing the wounds of his prisoners and feeding them in the middle of the night (Acts 16:33–34). Saul of Tarsus, who had persecuted the Christians for their faith, had an encounter with Jesus, and later volunteered to die for the same faith (Acts 9; 2 Tim. 4:6).

Born-again life has evidence. Spirit-filled life has evidence. There are spiritual manifestations evidencing real transformation of people and situations as a result of the infilling of the Spirit. The gifts of the Spirit and the fruits of the Spirit manifest as a consequence of the work of the Spirit. Real changes accompany true conversion and baptism in the Holy Spirit.

Godly life manifests most obviously in the decisions and choices Christians make. Our choices become evidence of our walk with God. Actually, the Bible gives many examples of both bad and good choices people made. The following are some examples to compare and contrast unhealthy and healthy choices.

In the Old Testament, Cain's decision to worship with a wrong motive was a bad choice with a bad outcome (Gen. 4:2–8). So was Esau's decision to sell his birthright (Gen. 25:29–34). Samson's confession to Delilah was not a good choice (Judg. 16:15–19). King Saul's decision to keep the enemy alive against the prophet's instruction was a bad choice (1 Sam. 15:17–23). In the New Testament, we meet the rich young ruler, who made the decision to walk away from the kingdom of God (Matt. 19:16–22). What a poor choice he made! Hopefully, he came back at a later time, but we don't know that for sure. Demas, who forsook Paul because he fell in love with the world, is another example of a person who made a poor choice (2 Tim. 4:10). Governor Felix, who postponed a decision to put his faith in Christ because he could not see beyond his immediate goals, made a very poor choice (Acts 24:24–26). His words became part of the history of lost people, "That's enough for now! You may leave. When I find it convenient, I will send for you" (Acts 24:25). As far as we know, he never found it convenient.

There are better choices one can make that will demonstrate and contribute to a wholesome life. Let me share with you some of the decisions and choices you can make with God's help that will demonstrate, ensure, and enhance your health and well-being. These are choices a Christian can make without much effort.

Let me remind you before presenting these choices that wholeness is not earthly perfection; it is a dynamic state of being whole by faith. A whole person may have challenges in some area of his or life, but still lives by faith and enjoys the gift of wholeness. Wholeness has to do with salvation, peace, and harmony. The Old Testament concept of *shalom* (Hebrew word) and the New Testament concept of salvation (*soteria* in Greek) express true wholeness. Oral Roberts used to say that wholeness is holiness. I believe there is a connection between healing, wholeness, and holiness.

First, unity is a better choice than division. Whether it is in a family or a church, unity is a healthier choice. Where there are division and strife, there are also pain and sorrow. "How good and pleasant it is when God's people live together in unity" (Ps. 133:1). From the first family on earth, described in Genesis, to the current, postmodern family, disunity breeds dysfunction. The results always include mutual blame, increased shame, and lack of trust between members. Remember how Adam blamed Eve and she blamed the serpent? From my experience as a pastoral counselor, I can testify that blame, shame, and mistrust are still characteristics of dysfunctional families.

Forgiveness is a better choice than bitterness. As a chaplain working with various types of patients, I have seen unforgiveness make people sick and forgiveness bring them healing. I still remember a woman who was admitted to the City of Faith Hospital with a symptom of vomiting blood. Her symptoms remained unexplained after all sorts of tests were conducted for ulcers, cancer, lung disease, and so forth. At their wits' end, the doctors assigned a Christian psychologist and me as a chaplain to counsel and work with this woman. We spent considerable time counseling this woman regarding a very deep hurt in her life and praying with her. I clearly remember the day when she said in front of the doctors, nurses, and others that she was forgiving someone very close to her who had caused her much pain for many years. Within hours of that testimony, her major symptom—vomiting blood—stopped. No one knew how to explain it. I am sure that the medical profession did an excellent job, but her Christian doctors told me that her willingness to forgive had much to do with the good outcome. In a similar case, I read the testimony of a pastor whose unexplained chest pains disappeared after he forgave his associate.

Forgiveness is actually a choice; it is an act of the will to begin with. It is a spiritual act done by faith. This is why the Lord taught us to pray, "And forgive us our debts, as we also have forgiven our debtors" (Matt. 6:12). I do not believe that forgiveness requires forgetting the events behind the hurt because forgiveness is a spiritual matter and remembering is an act of the brain. Ultimately, one may forget, but the most important thing is to decide to forgive. Even when one remembers the events behind the hurt, a forgiving person can expect to remember with less or no pain.

Holding on to bitterness only hurts us. It is like guarding someone in a ditch; you cannot do it without being stuck at the edge of the ditch with him. We need to move on.

I received a letter once from a sender whose name I did not recognize on the envelope. I did recognize her as soon as I read the note inside: "I have felt impressed in the last few months to write you to express my sorrow for having caused you pain as a young pastor. Please forgive me. Heb. 13:17." This was a church member who had given me unexplained grief when I was a fresh-out-of-divinity-school, twenty-four-year-old pastor of a New England church. At the time, I had no idea why she was giving me a hard time for no good reason, but I did not pick a fight with her. Apparently, she did not know why she was acting that way either. I received this letter three decades after I'd left that church. People do change, often for the better. It is better to release them whether they change or not. I was fortunate to have let go long ago without holding on to my hurt feelings. I am glad she worked things out with the Lord and me, but if I had held on to the hurt feeling, I would have wasted a lot of time and energy. I did send a comforting reply to her note. Forgiveness is possible, and its long-term outcome is wonderful. I once had a seminary student who went to the local prison to announce to her father's murderer that she had forgiven him!

Holiness is a better choice than worldliness. I believe there is such a thing as spiritual gravity, which is the aggregate weight of the world, the flesh, and the devil that pulls us down in our spiritual life. At the same time, unlike the earth's gravity, with spiritual gravity, we as believers have a choice in the matter because greater is he that is in us than he that is in the world (1 John 4:4). We can claim holiness and resist the spiritual gravity by depending on the grace of God. I am not referring to some superficial appearance of holiness here. I mean real, God-centered holiness that actually begins on the inside of a believer and works its way outward, eventually manifesting outside. This type of holiness is a better choice than worldliness, which leads to destruction.

Love is a better choice than hate. We are instructed to love even our enemies and to pray for our persecutors. Listen to Jesus:

> "You have heard that it was said, 'Love your neighbor and hate your enemy.' But I tell you, love your enemies and pray for those who persecute you, that you may be children of your Father in heaven. He causes his sun to rise on the evil and the good, and sends rain on the righteous and the unrighteous. If you love those who love you, what reward will you get? Are not even the tax collectors doing that?" (Matt. 5:43–46)

The apostle John, in his final messages, advised us to love one another (1 John 4:7–8). We are capable of loving even our enemies and making a choice to love. I will never forget the testimony of a pastor from the Fiji islands I heard several years ago at a conference in Oklahoma City. His ancestors had been man-eaters until the gospel of Jesus came to his island. He said that today the island is welcoming outsiders with open arms because the gospel taught them to love people instead of killing them. The power of the gospel is real.

We are empowered to love others. We can love because we are loved. We love God because He first loved us. Jesus expressed his love for us by giving Himself for us while we were still sinners. In Paul's words, now "the love of God is shed abroad in our hearts by the Holy Ghost which is given unto us" (Rom.

5:5 KJV). John added, "There is no fear in love. But perfect love drives out fear, because fear has to do with punishment. The one who fears is not made perfect in love" (1 John 4:18).

Happiness is a better choice than misery. People are often surprised to find out that they can choose happiness. Happiness is not something that happens to us; it can be a choice. The apostle Paul was in dire circumstances when he wrote to the Philippians, advising them to "rejoice in the Lord always. I will say it again: Rejoice" (Phil. 4:4)! I have seen believers in India who live in very poor economic situations demonstrating the kind of joy that Paul was talking about. Their possessions are not the source of their joy. I can assure you that the joy of the Lord is their strength (Neh. 8:10). Those of us who live in affluent societies can learn a lesson from these brothers and sisters about choosing to rejoice. I have been convicted of my own exaggerated misery when I am with these Christians. Let us exercise our ability to choose happiness in all circumstances.

Serving is a better choice than bossing people around. I have seen my share of toxic leaders in the Christian community. I have witnessed some who love to lord it over God's people instead of serving them. Service is a choice. True leaders are servant leaders who choose to take the basin and towel in the name of Christ. Serving one another and serving the Lord are choices. That is why Joshua told the people of Israel:

> "But if serving the LORD seems undesirable to you, then choose for yourselves this day whom you will serve, whether the gods your ancestors served beyond the

Euphrates, or the gods of the Amorites, in whose land you are living. But as for me and my household, we will serve the LORD." (Josh. 24:15)

As whole persons, we can choose to serve our God and serve others in His name. When we serve the "least of these," we are serving our Lord and Master. "Truly I tell you, whatever you did for one of the least of these brothers and sisters of mine, you did for me" (Matt. 25:40).

Healing is a better choice than brokenness. According to the Bible, we have much to do with our own health and well-being. Healing for Christians is not magical. It is natural and supernatural at the same time. Oral Roberts used to say that we live in a continuum between the natural and the supernatural realms. We have the capacity to move within this continuum. God has built into our natural bodies many healing capacities. We also have a spiritual dimension that transcends the body. Of course, there are things beyond our control, but we are not without any control. For instance, diet and exercise matter, and the quarantines prescribed in the Old Testament have their place in our lives still. There are also spiritual diets and exercises we can implement.

Sometimes our decisions have a more direct bearing on our healing and wholeness. Remember the man in John 5 who had been sick for thirty-eight years? He was at the pool of Bethesda for nearly four decades. This was the place where people got healed if they jumped into the pool when an angel stirred up the water. Whoever made it in time would be healed.

This lame man seemed to have had no chance in all these years. When we listen to his conversation with Jesus, we realize that he had a really mixed-up theology of healing. It seems that he believed that healing came only the way with which he was familiar. He also believed that he was in competition with others for his healing, which is understandable considering his almost forty years of experience at the pool. He had spent a lot of time waiting for an angel or a man to help him, but instead of an angel or a man, Jesus Himself—the Maker of angels and men—came to visit him one day.

Jesus came to that pool and engaged in a conversation with the man by asking a strange question: "Do you want to be healed?" Amazing! A sick man who was at a healing place for thirty-eight years was being asked if he really wanted to be healed. Amazingly, he was not offended. It appears that he had a choice in the matter of his healing.

The man gave his story, but then Jesus told him to take up his bed and walk. We are told that the invalid did exactly that. He took up his bed and walked.

This man was expecting his thirty-ninth year to be exactly like the previous thirty-eight, but that was not to be. He was given a choice and he took it.

Now, it is never wise to blame the patient for a lack of faith or healing, but all of us need to make sure that we truly choose healing and wholeness. It is sometimes very risky to choose healing because being healed means we lose the sympathy of our community. It may also mean that we will lose our sickbeds. The bed will not be carrying us anymore; instead, we will be carrying the bed as a testimony. It is a scary thought, but we must choose healing anyway! We are all afraid to lose that which carries us. Faith in Jesus means that we will risk it for the sake of healing and wholeness.

Let me conclude this chapter with two case studies from the Old Testament. This involves two characters who made important choices, one making unwise choices and the other one making healthy ones. Lot made three bad choices: (1) he chose things over people; (2) he chose to live at the edge of Sodom instead of in the promised Canaan; and (3) he pursued superficial water rather than re-dig the deep wells of his heritage.

Conversely, Lot's cousin Isaac, like his father, Abraham, chose (1) to live in temporary tents rather than in permanent dwellings, looking for a city whose builder and maker is God (Heb. 11:10); (2) he dug up old wells the enemies of his family had closed instead of depending on superficial rain or dry cisterns (Gen. 26:18); and (3) again, like his father, he built altars to worship Jehovah rather than the local idols (v. 25).

Lot's life did not end well, but Isaac is remembered as a patriarch. God is known as the God of Abraham, Isaac, and Jacob (Ex. 3:6, 15–16; 4:5, for example). Lot did not make the list. There is a lesson here for us. Our choices matter. We must be led by the Spirit and make godly choices. They will confirm God's work in us through the Holy Spirit and move us toward wholeness. God can turn our brokenness to wholeness. By faith, we can claim that we are whole persons.

Dear reader, by faith you are a whole person. Depend on the power of the Holy Spirit and walk by faith in wholeness.

Questions for Reflection

1. List the names of some Old Testament characters whose lives were transformed as a result of an encounter with God.
2. List the names of individuals in the New Testament whose lives changed similarly.
3. List some of the healthy choices people in the Bible made as an indication of their changed lives.
4. How would you define wholeness?
5. What are the seven healthy choices recommended in this chapter?
6. Which of these is more challenging in your life?
7. What have you learned from the choices Lot made?
8. What are the lessons you see in the choices Isaac made?
9. Are there some important decisions and choices facing you now?
10. What is the Lord saying to you about those?

Part 2

Discover Your Purpose in God's Call

A Word about the Idea of God's Call

Many Christians believe that the call of God applies only to ordained ministers and others in full-time Christian service. This is a profound misunderstanding, and it costs much to God's work in the world, as it eliminates a great number of God's people from purposefully serving God. God's call is a definite pre-requirement for Christian ministers who serve in various ministry offices, such as, apostle, prophet, evangelist, pastor, and teacher. However, the call of God is not limited to people who consider Christian ministry as their career or vocation. All Christians are called by God for His purposes.

People called to the ordained ministry go through a process of discovery and confirmation. Richard Niebuhr, for instance, taught that a call to the ordained ministry has four stages: (1) *the call to be a Christian*, (2) a *secret call* when the person has a sense of calling but no one else knows about it, (3) a *providential call* when the called person's gifts and talents are revealed naturally, and finally (4) the recognition of God's call on the person by the body of Christ by ordination, which Niebuhr calls the *ecclesiastical call*.[16] This is a very traditional view of God's call to ministry, and I affirm it. However, having been a pastor, chaplain, and seminary dean, I now believe that God's call as a process applies to all believers, not just professional ministers. In fact, except for Niebuhr's fourth stage, the process may be the same for all Christians. For those who are not ordained ministers, the fourth stage of recognition of the call may be informal or by those outside the church.

I believe God calls all of us to live out our lives as expressions of our relationship to Him, our position as disciples of Jesus Christ, and as citizens of the kingdom of God. I believe Paul held this view. His admonition to the Colossians and Thessalonians support this:

> And whatever you do, whether in word or deed, do it all in the name of the Lord Jesus, giving thanks to God the Father through him. (Col. 3:17)
>
> In the name of the Lord Jesus Christ, we command you, brothers and sisters, to keep away from every believer who is idle and disruptive and does not live according to the teaching you received from us. (2 Thess. 3:6)

Paul saw a Christian's life as his service and ministry.

It is important for us to discover our purpose by discerning God's call on our lives. We are all called to bring glory to God

---

16 H. Richard Niebuhr, *The Purpose of the Church and Its Ministry* (New York: Harper and Brothers, 1956), 64.

through our life and work. It does not matter whether one is a preacher or a plumber; both must serve God and fulfill His purposes through their work. We fulfill our purpose by finding and fulfilling God's purpose for us. This section presents our identity as it relates to our purpose. Read it with a desire to discover or affirm your purpose.

Chapter 6

⋀ ⋀ ⋀

You are a Healer, Serving a Wounded Healer

"Heal the sick, raise the dead, cleanse those who have leprosy, drive out demons. Freely you have received; freely give."

—Matthew 10:8

As a follower of Jesus Christ, you are called to be a healer, one who believes in and offers natural and supernatural healing. Have you thought about this awesome challenge and privilege?

There are two types of Christians in the world. The first group, called *cessationists*, believes that miracles have ceased. According to them, either around AD 150, when the last apostle died, or by AD 350, when the New Testament canon was completed, the miracles ceased. Since we now have the word of God in the form of the Bible, we no longer need signs and wonders or healings and miracles, they say. Cessationists consider these supernatural occurrences divine interventions that the primitive church needed to establish itself. Now that the church is established and mature, these are no longer necessities.

There are many misconceptions associated with the cessationist view. Here are just a few:

* Sin is the cause of all sicknesses.
* We are sanctified through sickness.
* With the progress and provisions of medical science, there is no need for signs and wonders today.
* Miracles are primitive and represent an unscientific worldview.
* There are no demons, only evil.
* Only the gifted few can minister healing.
* Healing ministers generally are dishonest and self-serving people.
* Sickness is always a cross to bear.
* Only saints can work miracles.

Obviously, these are not sound positions. Unfortunately, these are mainstream teachings today.

The second group is called *continualists*. They review the biblical teaching and the history of the church and conclude that signs and wonders and miracles are normative for the church in all ages. Highly regarded scholars such as Craig Keener of

Asbury Theological Seminary are in this group. Continualists define *miracle* as the manifestation of God's power and healing to make broken people whole.

Here are some reasons continualists believe in healing and miracles:

* Healing of the sick is a biblical idea.
* Jesus healed the sick.
* The disciples healed the sick.
* Seventy people sent out by Jesus healed people.
* Jesus commissioned his disciples to heal the sick.
* The apostles who followed the Twelve healed the sick.
* The early church practiced healing (James 5:14–16).
* Church history testifies to the healing ministry of the church.

I have been involved with the healing ministry of the church for a number of years. In addition to being involved with the ministry of Oral Roberts, I have participated in the healing work of the church as a pastor, chaplain, and guest minister in and outside the United States. Let me share with you my understanding of the healing ministry of Jesus.

Jesus commanded His disciples to minister healing. "Jesus called his twelve disciples to him and gave them authority to drive out impure spirits and to heal every disease and sickness." He said, "As you go, proclaim this message: 'The kingdom of heaven has come near.' Heal the sick, raise the dead, cleanse those who have leprosy, drive out demons. Freely you have received; freely give" (Matt. 10:1, 7–8). To the disciples, healing was the sign that the kingdom of God had arrived. Jesus announced, "If it is by the Spirit of God that I drive out demons, then the kingdom of God has come upon you" (Matt. 12:28). When the followers of John the Baptist asked, "Are you the one who is to come, or should we expect someone else?" Jesus replied, "Go back and report to John what you hear and see: The blind receive sight, the lame walk, those who have leprosy are cleansed, the deaf hear, the dead are raised, and the good news is proclaimed to the poor. Blessed is anyone who does not stumble on account of me" (Matt. 11:3–6). Healing meant that Jesus was the Messiah He claimed to be.

The Gospels present at least twenty-two distinct instances of physical healings. The list of disorders He healed is long:

* leprosy (Matt. 8:2)
* paralysis (Matt. 8:6)
* muteness (Matt. 9:32)
* blindness and lameness (Matt. 15:30)
* fever (Mark 1:30–31)
* bleeding (Mark 5:25)
* deafness (Mark 7:32)
* crippling deformity (Luke 13:11)
* dropsy (Luke 14:2 KJV), or edema

Other scriptures indicate healing of "every disease" (Matt. 10:1), "various diseases" (Mark 1:34), and "various kinds of sickness" (Luke 4:40).

Thomson K. Mathew

Jesus used various methods to heal the sick. He healed the sick by *speaking* to them: "When he saw them, he said, 'Go, show yourselves to the priests.' And as they went, they were cleansed" (Luke 17:14). He healed people by *touching* them: "Jesus . . . touched the man's ear and healed him" (Luke 22:51). Matthew talks about the two blind men who called out to Jesus. Jesus asked them, "What do you want me to do for you?" "Lord," they answered, "we want our sight." Matthew reports, "Jesus had compassion on them and touched their eyes. Immediately they received their sight and followed him" (Matt. 20:32–34). It appears that those Jesus touched as well as those who touched Jesus got healed (Matt. 9:20; 14:34–36). Jesus used the unusual means of *spitting* to heal people (Mark 8:22–25; John 9:6). The early church *anointed with oil* as a method of healing: "Is anyone among you sick? Let them call the elders of the church to pray over them and anoint them with oil in the name of the Lord. And the prayer offered in faith will make the sick person well; the Lord will raise them up. If they have sinned, they will be forgiven" (James 5:14–15).

Often our discussions of healing are limited to physical healing. This is a mistake. Divine healing is not limited to physical healing of the body. God wants to heal all areas of our lives, body, mind, and spirit. God's healing reaches out to other areas of our lives, such as relationships and finances. Healing has to do with our brokenness. God wants to heal all our brokenness and sorrows. It is high time for our culture in general and the body of Christ in particular to give up the stigmatization of emotional and mental disorders. Brokenness requires healing regardless of its location. Because we are fearfully and wonderfully made, brokenness in one area affects other areas of our lives. Physicians have proven that matters of the mind affect the body, and vice versa. We must not hesitate to pray for healing of brokenness in the mind or the spirit. Jesus made this point when He said, "Which is easier: to say to this paralyzed man, 'Your sins are forgiven,' or to say, 'Get up, take your mat and walk'? But I want you to know that the Son of Man has authority on earth to forgive sins" (Mark 2:9–10). Just as sickness in one area affects other areas of our lives, healing in one area also affects other areas. True healing is wholeness.

Considering all illnesses as directly related to personal sins is another mistake many make in the body of Christ. This approach will only cause us to give and receive condemnation. Sin and sickness do not always have a cause-effect relationship. Often the sinfulness of this fallen world, not our personal sins, is the basis of our sicknesses. We must be careful judging sick people by labeling them as sinners. When Jesus met sick people, there was no name-calling; He offered them compassion, not condemnation. We must learn to imitate Jesus in this matter. May compassion well up in us as we encounter other people's pain and suffering.

As I mentioned in chapter 4, we live in the between. We live between the kingdom that has come and the kingdom that is yet to come. We live between ordinary time (*chronos*) and God's fullness of time (*kairos*), somewhere on the natural-supernatural continuum. We certainly appreciate the contributions and healing work of physicians, nurses, and other health professionals.

We are grateful for research-based medicine that helps humanity. But these blessings should not discredit the privilege of divine healing. We should expect and thank God for signs, wonders, healings, and miracles when they occur. Oral Roberts used to say that God heals naturally and supernaturally: God used both Luke the physician and Paul the missionary to heal people. Oral Roberts also said that God heals in three ways: instantly, gradually, and ultimately in the resurrection.

We can receive healing as a sign of the kingdom of God and as a gift of the Holy Spirit. Professor Howard Ervin, an esteemed colleague, believed that healing is a sign of the kingdom of God and God's love gift to His children. Signs confirm the preaching of the kingdom of God. They give a foretaste of the kingdom of God yet to be fulfilled. We are kingdom people now and can enjoy this benefit of our kingdom citizenship. At the same time, the Holy Spirit dwells in us, working in us and through us, and enabling us to receive healing for ourselves and minister healing to others. We can expect healing to manifest as a gift of the Holy Spirit for us and others.

Paul said that we are sealed by the Holy Spirit (Eph. 1:13 KJV). The Holy Spirit is called the firstfruits, meaning, more fruits are to come (Rom. 8:23). The Holy Spirit is the earnest or down payment of our full redemption. The full purchase will come. The Holy Spirit works internally to sanctify us (Rom. 15:16) and externally to empower us for specific tasks (Acts 4:8, 31). The gifts of healing have to do with the internal and external work of the Spirit in our lives.

Divine healing requires faith, but it is not as many Christians think. Let's examine this carefully. Jesus did look for faith. That's why He asked the blind men, "Do you believe that I am able to do this?" When they said yes, Jesus told them, "According to your faith will it be done to you" (Matt. 9:28–29). He commended people for their faith. To the Canaanite woman He said, "Woman, you have great faith! Your request is granted" (Matt. 15:28). He rebuked His disciples for their lack of faith. Jesus' words were strong when the man with the sick son told Him His disciples could not heal him: "You unbelieving and perverse generation," Jesus chided. "How long shall I stay with you and put up with you? Bring your son here" (Luke 9:41). The disciples requested Jesus to increase their faith (Luke 17:5). Matthew tells us that Jesus could not do many miracles in his hometown because of their lack of faith (Matt. 13:57–58).

There is, however, another side to this matter. For instance, faith is not mentioned in the case of the lame man who had been at the pool of Bethesda for thirty-eight years (John 5:1–8). The man who was brought down the roof in Mark 2 is not reported to have faith, but we can imagine that the people who brought him had tremendous faith to do what they did (vv. 1–12). We cannot argue that on the day Lazarus was raised from the dead, he was full of faith! What is the point? The point is that the burden of faith is not on the patient; it is on the community of faith. Patients need faith; however, it is wrong to blame the patient for any lack of healing. There are times when the community surrounding the patient must stand in the gap and believe God for healing. After all, we are not asked to have a ton of faith. It takes much less. "Truly I tell you, if you have faith as small as a mustard seed, you can say to this mountain, 'Move from here to there,' and it will move. Nothing will be impossible for you" (Matt. 17:20).

We are saved from sin by faith in Jesus Christ. We are also healed by faith in Jesus Christ. Healing was prophesied centuries ago by Isaiah. "Surely he took up our pain and bore our suffering, yet we considered him punished by God, stricken by him, and afflicted" (Isa. 53:4). Listen to the testimony of the fulfillment of this promise in Matthew: "When evening came, many who were demon-possessed were brought to him, and he drove out the spirits with a word and healed all the sick. This was to fulfill what was spoken through the prophet Isaiah: 'He took up our infirmities and bore our diseases' (8:16–17). In the name of Jesus, there is salvation and healing. As Howard Ervin used to say, saving faith is healing faith and healing faith is saving faith. We can say amen to Peter when he says, "By His stripes we are healed" (1 Peter 2:4, paraphrased).

I have reviewed the biblical teaching on healing in this chapter to remind you that you are a healer. You not only have the privilege to receive healing in your life, but you also can minister healing to others in the name of Jesus. You can stand in the gap by faith for others' healing. You can touch a hurting life and make a difference. It is not anything magical. It is your right and privilege as a citizen of the kingdom of God and as a person filled with the Holy Spirit. As a witness of the kingdom of God, you can expect God to confirm His word with signs, wonders, miracles, and healings. You can also expect God's healing as a gift of the Holy Spirit. You don't have to reject any of the natural means of healing to do this ministry. In fact, this ministry makes you a partner with doctors, nurses, and other people involved in the healing arts. Actually, it has nothing to do with you. It has everything to do with God's love and power—the real reason Jesus came down from heaven. The enemy comes to steal, kill, and destroy, but Jesus came to give us abundant life (John 10:10). Healing is part of the abundant life. You have been saved and set free to offer this life to others.

You don't have to be an official minister to do this work. Find a way to be a healer in your work or profession. You don't have to look or act religious to do this. Discover a way to minister healing appropriate to your community and context. You don't have to be a perfect person to be involved in this work. You don't have to be in perfect health either. You just have to walk by faith in Jesus. You represent Jesus, the wounded Healer. He has saved you and set you free to minister healing to others. Just know who you are and walk in that knowledge and authority. You are a healer, and like your Lord, a wounded healer. Claim your identity and walk in that authority in the name of Jesus.

Questions for Reflection

1. What are the basic teachings of the cessationists?
2. What are the teachings of the continualists?
3. Where do you find yourself in this division, and why?
4. Do you have any unresolved questions regarding your position?
5. What methods of healing did Jesus use?
6. What does this chapter say about faith and healing?
7. What are the two main reasons you can expect signs, wonders, healing, and miracles?
8. How would you connect the kingdom of God and the gifts of the Spirit with personal healing and a ministry of healing?
9. Is there an area in your life that needs healing?
10. Take a moment to pray for your own and/or someone else's healing.

Chapter 7

▲ ▲ ▲

You are a Believer, Worshipper, and Hope-Bearer

However, I admit that I worship the God of our ancestors as a follower of the Way, which they call a sect. I believe everything that is in accordance with the Law and that is written in the Prophets, and I have the same hope in God as these men themselves have, that there will be a resurrection of both the righteous and the wicked.

—Acts 24:14–15

Paul was arrested for preaching the gospel. He was brought before the Jewish council called the Sanhedrin, but due to a fight between the two factions of Jews (the Pharisees and the Sadducees), he was brought back to the barrack, and later presented before Governor Felix in Caesarea. The following major charges against him were read as the accusers waited impatiently for a verdict favorable to them.

1. The accused is a troublemaker
2. He is a rioter.
3. He desecrated the temple a few days ago.

Once the charges were formally read, based on Roman law, the governor had to allow the accused to make his defense. As he condescendingly motioned Paul to speak, the apostle made a brief but comprehensive statement in his defense. Following is a portion of that statement.

> You can easily verify that no more than twelve days ago I went up to Jerusalem to worship. My accusers did not find me arguing with anyone at the temple, or stirring up a crowd in the synagogues or anywhere else in the city. And they cannot prove to you the charges they are now making against me. However, I admit that I worship the God of our ancestors as a follower of the Way, which they call a sect. I believe everything that is in accordance with the Law and that is written in the Prophets, and I have the same hope in God as these men themselves have, that there will be a resurrection of both the righteous and the wicked. So I strive always to keep my conscience clear before God and man. (Acts 24:11–16)

The crowd waited to see the governor's response as he pondered the words he heard from the disliked preacher.

It looks as though Paul denied all charges and called them baseless, but then he confessed to some self-imposed charges. He said that he was not a troublemaker, rioter, or desecrator of the temple, but he believed all that was written in the Law and the prophets, he shared the hope of the resurrection of the dead, he strove to keep a clear conscience, and he worshipped God as a follower of the way of Jesus.

In other words, Paul made the following confessions.

* I am guilty of faith.
* I am guilty of worship.
* I am guilty of hope.

Notice that in his moment of crisis, Paul was boldly declaring his identity.

* I am a man of faith.
* I am a worshipper.
* I am a man of hope.

Guilty of faith. Paul was guilty of believing God's word. He believed God's word about His love for us. He believed the word of God about Christ being our savior, healer, and redeemer. He believed that Christian life begins and ends in faith. We are saved by faith (Eph. 2:8); we live by faith (Rom. 1:17); and we die in faith (Heb. 11:13). He also believed that Christ would come again (see 1 Thess. 4:13–15).

Paul knew the Scriptures. He knew that Abel had worshipping faith (Heb. 11:4). He knew that Enoch had walking faith and Noah had working faith (Gen. 5:24; 6:22). Paul was on a journey of faith that could only be described as life-surrendering faith. He said, "I know whom I have believed, and am convinced that he is able to guard what I have entrusted to him until that day" (2 Tim. 1:12). Indeed, he was guilty of faith; He was a man of faith.

Guilty of worship. Man was made to worship God. Worship is built into our design. We will worship something or someone, but whom we will worship is our choice. David the psalmist encouraged himself and others to worship God and to give Him thanks (Ps. 103:1; 107:1).

The apostle Paul was a worshipper. In his letter to the Romans, he gave us many reasons to worship. We worship because we are forever loved with an unconditional love. Listen to the apostle:

Who shall separate us from the love of Christ? Shall trouble or hardship or persecution or famine or nakedness or danger or sword? . . . No, in all these things we are more than conquerors through him who loved us. For I am convinced that neither death nor life, neither angels nor demons, neither the present nor the future, nor any powers, neither height nor depth, nor anything else in all creation, will be able to separate us from the love of God that is in Christ Jesus our Lord. (Rom. 8:35–39)

We worship because there is no more condemnation for us (Rom. 8:1). We worship because there is no more defeat, as "we know that in all things God works for the good of those who love him, who have been called according to his purpose" (Rom. 8:28). We worship because death has been defeated: "Where, O death, is your victory? Where, O death is your sting?" (1 Cor. 15:55). Whether by silently making melody in one's heart or by singing hymns, psalms, and spiritual songs (Col. 3:16), we are to worship God. Worship is not limited to communal worship; hence, Sunday morning is not the only time a Christian should worship; worship is both corporate and private.

Jesus was a worshipper. He sang a hymn of thanksgiving (believed to be Psalm 107) with His disciples just before the most crucial moment in His life, in Gethsemane (Matt. 26:30). Paul was a man of worship (Eph. 5:19). And remember the Lord's admonition, "True worshipers will worship the Father in the Spirit and in truth, for they are the kind of worshipers the Father seeks" (John 4:23). According to John, location is not the issue in worship, and the methods of worship are unimportant, but Spirit and truth matter greatly.

We are worshippers. We must worship God with our bodies, minds, and spirits (Deut. 6:5). With the increasing professionalization of church music, we make the mega mistake of thinking that only the professionals onstage should be worshippers. In many places, the congregation acts like an audience. The congregation of God's people are not just an audience. We are a gathering of saints who are actual participants in worship. The truth is that everyone, onstage and offstage, is onstage. There is only One in the audience. His name is Jesus, who is present wherever two or three are gathered in His name (Matt. 18:20).

Guilty of hope. Paul was a man of hope, living with both finite and infinite hope. His letters are hope-filled even when written while he was in dire circumstances. Hope for Paul was built on fulfilling the purposes of God. He believed that nothing would rob God of His plans, so as one involved in God's plans, he could follow a course with hope to see them fulfilled. Whether it involved reuniting with his friends or sharing the gospel in a new territory, Paul lived with hope. And concerning eternity, he was full of anticipation. Though committed to fulfill God's purpose for him in the flesh, he wanted to be with Christ. To be absent from the body was to be present with Christ, he said (2 Cor. 5:8 KJV). He lived in his body as a person of hope and looked forward to a life everlasting.

Paul expected the trumpet to sound at any moment for the resurrection of the dead, but lived as if he had more time to serve. His hope was not in any future events or dates; it was always in a person—Jesus Christ. Christ was his hope. Christ in us now is our hope (Col 1:27), according to Paul, but being with Christ in the future is also part of that hope. He was a man of hope who lived between hope already realized and hope yet to be fulfilled.

Paul was a hope-bearer. When I consider this idea of bearing hope, I think of my grandmother who used to live with us when I was a boy. Living in an Indian village where merchants carrying goods on their heads brought vegetables to the door, grandmother would often need to call back a seller who had gone past our home. Not knowing the name of the seller, she would call the person by whatever he or she was carrying. I have heard people respond to "Bananas" or "Coconuts!" not because that was their name, but because that was what they carried. We must remember that one is called by whatever he or she is carrying. Those who carry Christ are called Christians. They should also be called hope-carriers or hope-bearers because Christ in us is the hope.

As a chaplain, I have seen real hope bring healing to people. I have also seen hope prepare people for death in a very healthy way. I will never forget the missionary I met at the former City of Faith Hospital in Tulsa. This was a woman of God near ninety years old who had spent her entire life as a missionary in China and India. I did not know her personally until I met her as a patient at the City of Faith. Because of my roots in India, we developed a special relationship within a short time. As I entered her room one day, I noticed that she was in bed with her eyes closed but with a big smile on her face, as if she were looking at someone she had not seen in a long time. Her nurse and a missionary companion were standing by the bed quietly. All of a sudden she said, "Good night, everyone." We looked at each other in surprise, as it was only early afternoon. The sun was shining through the windows of the tall hospital building in Tulsa. I noticed that she did not say, "Good-bye." Then she spoke again, with her eyes still closed, smiling still: "Good night, everyone. It is morning up here!" As I realized the sacredness of the moment and pondered her words, within a few minutes she was gone to be with the Lord. I could only conclude that before she left her life on earth, she had a vision of the face of Jesus and a glimpse of the glory that was awaiting her. That missionary was a woman of hope. She had been a hope-bearer to many in China and India, and on that day she was seeing her own hope realized. I have been deeply impacted by her farewell words, by which she became a hope-bearer to me also.

Real hope knows that at any given moment of our lives, God has already been to the next moment. As Alpha and Omega, He has been to both the past and the future. He beckons us to come to join Him in the next moment of our lives. Following God's beckoning is a life of hope. A Christian will never enter a moment where God has not already been. We are never alone and we will never be alone. We don't have to live in fear and despair. We are people of hope. We are hope carriers. Christ is our hope. I have shared this thought with my daughters when they left home for higher studies. I wanted them to be fearless and hopeful as they entered the world of responsibilities and challenges away from home and parents. I share this with you today with the same desire.

Paul knew this. He was guilty of hope. He was a hope-bearer.

The Bible is a book of hope. Hope remains a major theme throughout the book, and the last chapter of Revelation ends in hope. Both the Old and the New Testaments bear witness to hope in God. There is much we can learn about who we are and how we should live in hope from this book of books. We will look at just one Old Testament book here—Habakkuk—which tells us how we should live hopefully in an age of terror.

It does not have the easiest or the fanciest name, but the book of Habakkuk contains a vital message of hope for our time.

Living like Habakkuk in the Age of Terror. What would you name the age in which we live? The age of globalization? The age of prosperity? The age of technology? All of these might be fitting names, but the fittest one is the age of terror.

I never thought we would live with the fear of terrorism in America, the land to which terrorized people from other nations have always fled for safety. This is still the land of the free and the home of the brave, but we have been profoundly affected by the events of September 11, 2001, and the turmoil around the world since then. From New Delhi to New York, people are concerned about terrorism and its impact on free societies.

There are those who believe that the underlying motivator of terrorism is the hopelessness of people in closed societies, especially in the Middle East. Until these masses find real hope in some form, terrorism will remain a threat to civilization. Who can forget the jetliner attack of the twin towers in New York City and the bombings of the commuter trains in Bombay, London, and Madrid?! No wonder, from high school campuses to high places of government, fear has become a significant factor in our lives.

It appears that we have learned to be more afraid than usual. Unfortunately, fear alienates. It affects mental health and spiritual well-being. Long-term fear will take its toll on us. How do we avoid this? How shall we live in a fearless way in these fearful times? Are there examples of such a way of living?

This is where Habakkuk can help us. He was a believer who lived in Jerusalem six hundred years before Christ. It is hard to believe that terrorism existed before our time. But the fact is that terrorists are not new on planet Earth. Only their methods have been updated. Habakkuk was an eyewitness to the horrors of terror.

Assyria was the ruling empire during his time. It was going down fast as a superpower. Egypt and Babylon were fighting to take the place left by Assyria. They wanted to be the next superpower. These were two powerful cultures in their day. Babylon won this fight in 605 BC, and Nebuchadnezzar became the ruler of the entire civilized world. He was the most powerful man on earth. Just seven years before, in 612 BC, Nineveh had fallen. Habakkuk lived and wrote during this turbulent period. His book describes a crisis moment in history.

Sounds familiar? Fall of empire! Fight for superpower status! Remember the Soviet Union and the fall of both the Iron Curtain and the Berlin wall? China wants to be the next superpower. The Russians would like to claim that title too. Clash of civilizations! We are familiar with this too now. Listen to Habakkuk. He sounds like one of our contemporary embedded war correspondents!

> How long, LORD, must I call for help, but you do not listen? Or cry out to you, "Violence!" but you do not save? Why do you make me look at injustice? Why do you tolerate wrongdoing? Destruction and violence are before me; there is strife, and conflict abounds. (Hab. 1:2–3)

Habakkuk was an eyewitness to multiplied injustices and conflicts, and he was so fed up that he had begun questioning God. "How can You stand it, God?" he wondered. "How could You allow this?"

> Your eyes are too pure to look on evil; you cannot tolerate wrong. Why then do you tolerate the treacherous? Why are you silent while the wicked swallow up those more righteous than themselves? (1:13)

Habakkuk described the anarchy of his day: "The law is paralyzed, and justice never prevails. The wicked hem in the righteous, so that justice is perverted" (1:4).

Habakkuk was very concerned about the political, social, and spiritual situation in which he found himself. His context was frightening. Idolatry seemed to be pervading his society. He was not a happy camper:

> Of what value is an idol, since a man has carved it? Or an image that teaches lies? For he who makes it trusts in his own creation; he makes idols that cannot speak. Woe to him who says to wood, "Come to life!" Or to lifeless stone, "Wake up!" Can it give guidance? It is covered with gold and silver; there is no breath in it. (Hab. 2:18–19)

His situation was dire, but to his utter despair, Habakkuk was expecting conditions to get worse. He was anticipating a worst calamity. Listen to him: "I heard and my heart pounded, my lips quivered at the sound; decay crept into my bones, and my legs trembled. Yet I will wait patiently for the day of calamity to come on the nation invading us" (Hab. 3:16).

Habakkuk was a man of strong faith, but he was overwhelmed. He had some serious questions for God. His questions and God's answers to them help us discover the way we ought to live at such a time as ours.

Asking questions is not the sign of a lack of faith. God is not offended by the questions His children raise. Habakkuk's questions can be divided into two general categories: First, the why questions; then the "how long" questions. Interestingly, God did not answer Habakkuk with neat answers, but He did tell Habakkuk how to live at such a time as his. How should a believer live with hope in violent times? The book of Habakkuk gives clear answers.

God is in Charge: God's first response to Habakkuk was that He was in charge of the world. Often we live as if someone other than God is in charge of the world and its history. God wanted Habakkuk to learn that "the earth is the LORD's, and everything in it, the world, and all who live in it" (Ps. 24:1). He wanted him to conclude, "The LORD is in his holy temple: let all the earth keep silence before him" (Hab. 2:20). This was an important lesson for Habakkuk to contemplate.

The lesson from Genesis to Revelation is that God is involved in His creation. He is in charge even when bad things seem to be happening, when unpleasant things seem to be out of control. God is in charge. This is true at all times. There is no time when God is not in charge.

It is natural for us to wonder about God's role in the world at times when world events are overwhelming to us. We want to make sense of the chaos around us. When things do not make any sense, we are prone to wonder about God's place in the world. This is especially true when we observe the suffering of the innocent. Why should a good God allow such bad things to happen? The fact is that we do not know the answer to that question fully yet, but we should not forget that most of the things that cause us to rail against God are created or done by us—God's creation entrusted with a free will!

God is in charge of life and everything about it. We can be sure that God's purposes are being accomplished in the world. We, along with Habakkuk, need to remember this in times of violence. We need to remember this when fear grips our souls. We also have to remember that the God who is in charge of the world is a good God. His goodness has no end. He is love. His love is everlasting. A good response to God on our part is to be like the psalmist and say: "Give thanks to the LORD, for he is good; his love endures forever" (Ps. 107:1).

Idols are not in charge of the world. "Of what value is an idol, since a man has carved it[?] . . . [It] cannot speak [because it is] . . . wood [or] lifeless stone[?] . . . Can it give guidance? . . . There is no breath in it" (Hab. 2:18–19). God is alive. He speaks. He guides His people. He is in charge.

This means the Taliban is not in charge. Al-Qaeda is not in charge. Jihadists are not in charge. Hamas is not in charge. Hezbollah is not in charge. In fact, even the United Nations is not in charge of the world. God is. Why should we then live in fear and hopelessness?

Live by Faith: The second answer Habakkuk gives us for how we should live in violent times is this: "The righteous person will live by his faith" (Hab. 2:4). We are constantly tempted to live by sight, but living based on what our eyes can see can be scary. Faith sees the invisible, believes the incredible, and accomplishes the impossible. To live without fear, we must learn to live by faith, whether in peacetime or times of conflict. Living by faith requires us to trust God and depend on Him. This is not easy for modern people. We want to depend on ourselves. We want to be secure and self-sufficient. But Habakkuk says there is no such thing as living by sight without fear.

The Bible contains the story of those who lived by faith and instructions on how to live like them. Hebrews 11 is an example of this. Enoch, Abraham, Isaac, Jacob, Joseph, and Moses are among those who were commended for their faith. There are also countless people whose names are not given, but their life of faith is described in detail.

[They] who through faith conquered kingdoms, administered justice, and gained what was promised; who shut the mouths of lions, quenched the fury of the flames, and escaped the edge of the sword; whose weakness was turned to strength; and who became powerful in battle and routed foreign armies. Women received back their dead, raised to life again. There were others who were tortured, refusing to be released so that they might gain an even better resurrection. Some faced jeers and flogging, and even chains and imprisonment. They were put to death by stoning; they were sawed in two; they were killed by the sword. They went about in sheepskins and goatskins, destitute, persecuted, and mistreated—the world was not worthy of them. They wandered in deserts and mountains, living in caves and in holes in the ground. (Heb. 11:33–38)

A life of faith is a life with triumphs and trials. It enables one to conquer kingdoms and receive back the dead, on the one hand. On the other hand, it may cause one to wander in deserts, mountains, caves, and holes in the ground or cause one to be sawed in two or stoned to death! It is clear that faith is not for wimps. It requires strength and courage. Living without fear requires living by faith. This day and age require such living.

Live by Hope: Habakkuk learned to live by hope. In the midst of utter chaos, he began to practice hope by declaring that "the earth will be filled with the knowledge of the glory of the LORD, as the waters cover the sea" (Hab. 2:14). Imagine! Violence surrounded the prophet. Injustices abounded. The wicked were flourishing. The innocent were suffering. But the prophet was a man of hope who saw by faith a time in the future when the knowledge of the glory of the Lord would fill the earth. It would be deep and wide and vast as the ocean.

We live in a world of hopeless people. Hopelessness is at the root of violence in many parts of the world today. The Middle East crisis, especially, needs to be examined in this regard.

Hopelessness creates suicide bombers. Bullets alone won't stop them permanently. Hope will.

Crisis times call us to be hope-bearers. Christians are called hope-carriers because we carry Christ in us. We know that "God has chosen to make known among the Gentiles the glorious riches of this mystery, which is Christ in you, the hope of glory" (Col. 1:27).

We learn from Paul and Habakkuk to live by hope, to find our identity as hope-bearers. Hear God's call on your life to be a hope-bearer in your context. Consider it your purpose to be a carrier of hope in this hopeless world. Walk in this identity as a bearer of hope in your personal life and "you will not fear the terror of night nor the arrow that flies by day" (Ps. 91:5).

Questions for Reflection

1. What were the main charges brought against the apostle Paul?
2. What were the confessions he made in response?
3. What were the identity statements Paul was making through his response to Governor Felix?
4. How would you define faith?
5. Why should we worship God?
6. How do you understand Christian hope?
7. What are the three lessons we receive from Habakkuk?
8. Is there an area of your life this chapter is specifically addressing?
9. What is the Lord saying to you about that area?
10. What resolutions would you consider?

Chapter 8

▲ ▲ ▲

You Are a Leader

*Sitting down, Jesus called the Twelve and
said, "Anyone who wants to be first must
be the very last, and the servant of all."*

—MARK 9:35

Once a well-known person told me, "I do not have headaches, Tom; I give headaches!" It is hard to believe, but
these were the words of a man who was in a position of leadership in a Christian organization. God has called us to be leaders
who are healers, not wounders. Many people, including some
in leadership, engage in wounding others instead of leading as
agents of healing and wholeness.

There is so much confusion about true leadership today and
a great shortage of capable and ethical leaders. The situation is

bad in business, industry, and politics alike. I must unwillingly confess that things are not much better in the world of religion.

There is so much talk about leadership today. Books on leadership abound to the point that I have recently complained to my colleagues about the need for having some books on *followership*. Indeed, much in the world depends on leadership, but a lot of things are left undone or unfinished in the world now because of a lack of statesman leaders. There was a time when we could easily name people who were giants in their fields, impacting the course of human history and the fate of nations. We used to consider ourselves standing on their shoulders. That is not the case today. We no longer have a Lincoln, Churchill, Gandhi, or Martin Luther King Jr. The world desperately needs new leaders. The church also needs capable and godly leaders. How do you develop such leaders in this age of social media and sensationalist journalism, with their capacity to conduct character assassinations so easily?

There is a significant difference between leadership and Christian leadership. True leadership from a Christian perspective is servant leadership; a true Christian leader must be a Spirit-empowered, Spirit-led, and spiritually formed person. The Bible has much to say about leadership. Let's take a brief look.

There is leadership in the Trinity. God the Father is a leader; He led His people. God the Son is a leader too; He has invited humankind to follow Him. God the Holy Spirit is a leader; we are called to be led by the Spirit (Rom. 8:14).

The list of human leaders in the Old Testament is very long. Abraham was a leader; he led his family out of a pagan land (Gen.

15:7). Joseph led the government of Egypt during a crisis (Gen. 42:6). Moses led his people from bondage to freedom (Ex. 15:22). Miriam led God's people in worship (Ex. 15:21). Joshua was a leader who was groomed by Moses (Josh. 1:5). Deborah was a prophetic leader, serving as a judge and prophetess (Judg. 4:4). David led as a man after God's own heart (1 Sam. 13:14). Elijah and Elisha were leaders representing two generations (1 Kings 19:19). Daniel was a distinguished leader in Babylon (Dan. 2:49).

There is no shortage of leaders in the New Testament. The apostles were leaders. Stephen and other deacons were leaders (Acts 6:3). Peter was a leading personality among the disciples (Mark 10:28). Paul was a leader who asked others to follow him as he followed Christ (1 Cor. 4:16; 11:1). Priscilla was a woman in leadership in the early church (Rom. 16:3). Timothy was a bicultural leader mentored by Paul (2 Tim. 1:5).

Great leaders are seen throughout church history. You will recognize these names: Saint Augustine, Thomas Aquinas, Martin Luther, John Calvin, John Wesley, Jonathan Edwards, Charles Finney, Charles Parham, William Seymour, Martin Luther King Jr., and Kathryn Kuhlman.

Generally speaking, all good leaders have certain noticeable qualities. They are people with a vision who are effective communicators. They are open, honest, and perceived as fair. They make decisions after taking input from others and demonstrate consistency. They are goal-oriented, able to stay focused, and open to feedback. They are available to their followers; demonstrate loyalty to them, and offer praise and recognition. They are also willing to change for the common good. These qualities are not limited to Christian leaders.

Good Christian leaders have several special qualities: they love people; they have a servant attitude; they are honest; they think big and see the bigger picture, but are willing to fight for the individuals in need; they build up people and offer their best to others.

I have met some outstanding leaders and some very disappointing ones during my career as a minister, professor, and seminary dean. In my opinion, the worst leaders are those who simply use people to build things. The best leaders, on the other hand, use things to build up people, who will in turn build great things for them. What I have noticed is that people who use up people for their grandiose goals ultimately lose both things and people. Those who use things to build up people ultimately keep both people and things. Unfortunately, I must say that some big things poor leaders have built had more to do with their own egos and need for self-validation than they did a vision from God. They have created many casualties.

Leadership transitions are hard to deal with, but often they are badly needed. I have noticed four types of leadership transitions in the Bible. I have seen all of these within the church world:

1) Transition due to lost vision and corruption: this caused the transfer of leadership from Eli to Samuel (1 Sam. 2:17–18; 3:10–19).

2) Transition due to disobedience and arrogance: this caused the transition from Saul to David (1 Sam. 15:11–19, 26).

3) Transition due to the aging of the current leader: this was the situation with Elijah and Elisha (I Kings 19:19–21; 2 Kings 2:11–14).

4) Transition due to a major project God wanted to accomplish: this was the case with Moses and Joshua in the Old Testament (Ex. 3:7–10; Josh. 1:1–2) and Paul in the New Testament (Acts 9:15–16).

Guillermo Maldonado, a graduate of Oral Roberts University Seminary and pastor of a megachurch in Miami, gives one of my favorite definitions of a ministry leader as "an individual with the ability to exert influence, to identify gifts and talents in others, and to guide them to the destiny God has for them."[17] Notice that leadership is not about the leader. Maldonado describes the leader as one who

* encourages with words of affirmation
* inspires instead of manipulates
* motivates with words of faith
* influences by being an example
* guides through vision and purpose
* mobilizes and brings people together
* activates and awakens dormant gifts in others

---

17 Guillermo Maldonado, *Leaders that Conquer* (Miami, FL: GM International, 2004), 40.

* persuades through passion and drive
* disciplines through correction for maturity[18]

Maldonado lists the qualifications of a leader as follows:

1. Discipline—self-control
2. Purpose—calling and destiny
3. Integrity—creates credibility
4. Vision—from God, not ambition
5. People skills—relational skills
6. Godliness—seeking God
7. Boldness—courage
8. Humility—gives glory to God
9. Decisiveness—vision-based
10. Loyalty—commitment/consistency[19]

Maldonado believes that a leader's success depends on his values. The following are some of the important values he has identified.

1. Gratefulness
2. Service
3. Respect for authority
4. Honoring of people's time
5. Teamwork
6. Promise keeping
7. Affirmation

---

18 Maldonado, 40—41.
19 Maldonado, 77—104.

8. Positive attitude
9. Peacemaking
10. Humility
11. Commitment to unity
12. Accountability
13. Transparency
14. Personal wholeness
15. Prayerfulness
16. Forethought
17. Truthfulness
18. Commitment to covenant[20]

I believe that Spirit-filled leadership has several unique require-ments. Spirit-filled leadership is service with power; we serve others in the name of Christ in the power of the Holy Spirit. It is true servant leadership and it requires: (1) an intimate encounter with God, (2) the anointing of the Holy Spirit, and (3) a willingness to take actions by faith as needed. Spirit-filled leadership is a walk by faith. Let me summarize my perspective on this below.[21]

Encounter with God
All godly leaders in Scripture experienced an intimate encounter with the living God. God met with Abraham personally (Gen. 17:1–6), and Moses encountered God on a mountainside in the

---

20 Maldonado, 183—199.
21 This section is adapted from my book *Spirit-Empowered Ministry in the 21st Century: Spirit-Led Preaching, Teaching, Healing and Leading* (Fairfax, VA: Xulon Press, 2004).

burning bush (Ex. 3:1–7). Joshua had an experience with God after Moses died (Josh. 1:1–5), and God revealed Himself to Samuel when he was a young man being discipled by Eli the priest (1 Sam. 3:4–11). Elijah encountered the word of God as he was commanded to go and hide himself by the brook Cherith (1 Kings 17:2–3 KJV). Isaiah encountered God the year King Uzziah died (Isa. 6:1–9), and Ezekiel met with God as the Lord asked him about the dry bones in the valley (Eze. 37:1–3).

An encounter with God is a life-transforming experience. Isaiah's experience demonstrates the framework of an encounter with God. First, Isaiah encounters the glory of God as He is seated high and lifted up in the temple. Immediately afterwards, Isaiah unexpectedly encounters impurity in himself. The unpleasantness of this confrontation causes him to cry out, "Woe is me. . . . I am a man of unclean lips!" (Isa. 6:5). Isaiah recognizes that his position as a prophet involves the use of his tongue, which is often found to be unclean, but God does not leave him in this condition of despair. God sends an angel with a red-hot coal to touch Isaiah's lips, and he is cleansed. After the cleansing process, he has an encounter with the call of God, when God asks, "Whom shall we send? And who will go for us?" Isaiah responds, "Here am I. Send me!" (v. 8).

Often leaders miss the second step of an encounter with God, which involves the acknowledgment of one's own inadequacies. Many overlook the mystery that God can use our weaknesses as well as our strengths. In fact, He can turn our weaknesses into strengths.

The lives of biblical leaders demonstrate that an encounter with God can truly transform a life. For instance, Abraham's life was changed in order to be a blessing to the nations, and Moses was transformed into the man who was to lead God's people out of bondage. Joshua was changed as God raised him up to lead them into the Promised Land. Samuel, Isaiah, Elijah, Ezekiel, and many others were also transformed through their encounters with the Lord.

A person's name is a significant part of his or her identity. Thus, when an individual's name is changed through an encounter with God, his or her identity is also changed. Jacob became Israel, Saul became Paul, and Simon became Peter.

An encounter with God also changes a person's agenda. The individual's goals are no longer important; he or she adopts God's goals. After the burning bush experience, Moses did not try to deliver the people his own way; he adopted God's way. The theme of a servant leader becomes, "Not my will, but thine."

Anointing of the Holy Spirit

Spirit-filled leadership requires the anointing of the Holy Spirit. "Anointing" here refers to the presence and power of God resting upon the leader. Personal qualities and abilities are not the most important aspects of a servant leader's work; the empowerment of the Holy Spirit makes the difference in one's service to others. The Bible clearly illustrates this. When King Saul disobeyed God, Samuel went to Bethlehem to anoint David as the next leader of the Israelites. Samuel invited Jesse and his sons to a place of worship (1 Sam. 16:3). Jesse's first son, Eliab, appeared to be an outstanding candidate, but the Lord said to Samuel, "Do not consider his appearance or his height . . . The LORD does not look at the things man looks at. Man looks at the outward appearance, but the LORD looks at the heart" (v. 7). Samuel was surprised as God rejected each of Jesse's seven sons and asked, "Are these all the sons you have?" When Jesse mentioned his youngest son, David, Samuel told him to send for David. When David approached, Samuel heard the Lord say, "'Rise and anoint him. This is the one.' So Samuel took the horn of oil and anointed him in the presence of his brothers, and from that day on the Spirit of the Lord came powerfully upon David" (vv. 11–13). David was selected by God and anointed by Samuel; the anointing brought the power of God into David's life.

Spirit-filled ministry is a powerful ministry. The power does not stem from personal charisma, but from the power of the Holy Spirit. The *charismata*, or gifts of the Holy Spirit, are more important than personality or personal charisma. The anointing of the Holy Spirit gives the unction for service, and the Holy Spirit empowers the servant leader.

Walk by Faith

It is one thing to receive the anointing of the Holy Spirit, but it is another matter to act on it. Christian leadership is a walk of faith. This faith walk is the door that allows the Holy Spirit to manifest Himself through the life and ministry of God's servants, and it is the anointing of the Holy Spirit that leads a minister to take action by faith. The relationship between Elijah and Elisha demonstrates this. After Elijah trained Elisha to become a prophet, the time came for Elijah to be taken from Elisha. The older prophet asked Elisha what he might do for him. Just as Solomon asked for wisdom, Elisha replied that he wanted a double portion of the Spirit that was upon Elijah. Although he could have asked for anything, Elisha asked for a double portion of the Spirit. Elijah responded that if Elisha were still around to see him depart, he would receive his wish.

Elisha followed Elijah from Gilgal to Bethel, from Bethel to Jericho, and from Jericho to the Jordan River. As Elisha watched, Elijah struck the Jordan with his mantle, and the river opened up for them to cross over to the other side. Soon after the senior prophet was taken up to heaven in a chariot of fire, his mantle fell to the ground. The mantle was a symbol of the anointing that was upon Elijah. Elisha picked up the mantle and held it in his hand as he stood by the river. As he struck the river with the mantle, he asked, "Where is the God of Elijah?" (2 Kings 2:14, paraphrased). Elisha had watched Elijah take many steps of faith; now the anointing that had rested upon Elijah had fallen upon him. It was time for him to act by faith.

As an act of pure faith, Elisha struck the water just as Elijah had, and it divided to the right and to the left! Spirit-filled servant leadership must involve walking and working by faith. The river would not have opened if he had just stood and waited. Striking the river was the first step of a great and powerful ministry.

The book of 2 Kings recounts the miracles Elisha performed. For example, when poisonous water was killing the land, Elisha cleansed it by adding salt (ch. 2). This miracle followed his first step of faith at the Jordan. Similarly, Elisha instructed Naaman, the deathly ill commander of the Syrian army, to immerse himself in the river seven times, and Naaman was healed (ch. 5). This healing would not have occurred if Elisha had merely stood by the river, holding the mantle in his hand. In the same manner, the widow whose sons were in danger of being enslaved received ministry and help from Elisha. She was obedient when the prophet instructed her to borrow vessels from her neighbors, and her obedience met the needs of her family (ch. 4). If Elisha had not taken the first step of faith in his ministry, the desperate needs of many would not have been met.

The key to success in power-filled servant leadership requires a true encounter with the living God, the anointing of the Holy Spirit, and the willingness to step out in faith.

Leaders are not formed instantly. The Bible speaks about several things happening "immediately," but leadership development is not one of them. Look at these verses:

* "Immediately he was cleansed of his leprosy" (Matt. 8:3).
* "Immediately they received their sight and followed him" (Matt. 20:34).
* "She came up behind him and touched the edge of his cloak, and immediately her bleeding stopped (Luke 8:44).

It does not say anywhere in the Bible that a leader was formed "immediately." God makes leaders through a process. At times it can be a painful process because in many ways it is a purifying process.

When Israel needed a leader like Moses to get them out of slavery, God had long before begun a process:

> A man of the tribe of Levi married a Levite woman, and she became pregnant and gave birth to a son. When she saw that he was a fine child, she hid him for three months. But when she could hide him no longer, she got a papyrus basket for him and coated it with tar and pitch. Then she placed the child in it and put it among the reeds along the bank of the Nile. His sister stood at a distance to see what would happen to him. (Ex. 2:1–4).

We know the rest of the story. No shortcut was involved.

When God was fed up with the corruption in Eli's household and wanted to bring in new leadership, He started a process with a barren woman named Hannah who later showed up with a child at Eli's door, saying, "Pardon me, my lord. As surely as you live, I am the woman who stood here beside you praying to the Lord. I prayed for this child, and the Lord has granted me what I asked of him. So now I give him to the Lord. For his whole life he will be given over to the Lord" (1 Sam. 1:26–28). That child, named Samuel, inherited Eli's leadership.

When the world needed Jesus to deliver it from sin, God did not start with Mary and Joseph. He had already begun with a Moabite woman named Ruth: "Boaz took Ruth and she became his wife. When he made love to her, the Lord enabled her to conceive, and she gave birth to a son" (Ruth 4:13). Matthew continues the genealogy of Jesus: "Salmon the father of Boaz, whose mother was Rahab, Boaz the father of Obed, whose mother was Ruth, Obed the father of Jesse, and Jesse the father of King David. . . . And Jacob the father of Joseph, the husband of Mary, and Mary was the mother of Jesus who is called the Messiah" (Matt. 1:5–6, 16). God had a strategic plan.

There are no fully made leaders. A leader is always in the making. A leader is often God's solution to some problem. The leader may not even know what that problem might be in the beginning of the call to leadership. In fact, a problem may not even exist when God begins the creation and development of a leader to solve it. Amazing!

God is now creating the solution to cancer, heart disease, terrorism, spiritual disintegration, a lost generation, dead religion, and other problems that may be only in the making. You may be a part of the solution to a preexisting problem or a big problem in the making.

You are a leader whether you have an official title or not. You are a leader whether you are a layperson or an ordained minister. You need to accept your leadership at the level God has given to you as a father, mother, homemaker, teacher, pastor, or whatever. Be patient. Be ready. Seek the anointing to match your calling. Your time is now or it is coming. In the meantime, you must walk with your head high and your spirit full.

I do not wish to lead you to believe that leadership requires the accomplishment of big tasks. The size and nature of the task are not the main issues in leadership. Leadership can manifest in small things and make a big difference in people's lives. Often it is not the big things we do or articulate that makes the biggest difference. There are small things that have a big impact.

The following e-mail I unexpectedly received as a Thanksgiving message from a man who was a teenager in a church I pastored in New England three decades ago illustrates the point. I share it as a humble testimony. I was a young pastor just out of the divinity school then. Somehow, God blessed the church and it grew to the point that we needed to build a new sanctuary. I normally think of the church growth we experienced, the building project, the mortgage burning for the land, and so on, as highlights of my leadership there; however, I never received any e-mail or letter regarding those matters from any church member. This e-mail (names changed for privacy) tells you what really mattered to one teenager.

> Greetings in the name of our Savior Jesus Christ!!. . . I hope this letter finds you filled with Holiday Joy.
>
> Get ready, I'm gonna tell you who I am . . . New Haven . . . mid 70s!!!!!! . . . I was a little boy, my name is Brian, I used to come to church with my foster family . . . My highlight memory with you was on a Sunday night service . . . for whatever reason you had all the teenagers . . . stand up!!!!! And every one of us gave a reason to be Thankful to The Lord [a Testimony] . . . of course as it would be, we sat front left as you looked off the Pulpit, 4 rows from the piano, and you started from the far right, so I stood there in agony!!!! the last

kid to speak!!! . . . I remember what I said! . . . and then you came and gave me a hug! . . . and to this day I not only remember it but it is still my Testimony . . . "I'd like to thank The Lord for Saving me and Raising me in a Christian Home" . . .

[A]s this season rolls through . . . you came to mind! and I felt it was time for another hug so HERE IT IS!!! . . . Sorry for the run on but Your name was on my heart and I looked you up and . . . if I never get a real hug here . . . I'll see you in Glory!! . . .
Happy Thanksgiving!!!!
Brian

My significant leadership contribution in this person's life was not church growth, a building project, or the mortgage burning, but a hug! The teenager who was living in a crowded foster home three decades ago remembers the most important aspect of my leadership to him—a simple embrace. Small things can be big when it comes to leadership!

It is possible that you are thinking of yourself as a person without many talents or much strength. Some of us think of ourselves as weak and wounded. You may want to think about what the late Henri Nouwen said about people who think and live that way. Nouwen was professor of pastoral care at Yale University Divinity School when I was a student there. One of his best-known works is titled *The Wounded Healer.*[22] The the-

---

22 Henri J. M. Nouwen, *The Wounded Healer: Ministry in Contemporary Society* (New York: Doubleday Image, 1979).

sis of this book is this: Jesus Christ is the true wounded healer. By His stripes we are healed. So also, God can use wounded Christians who are in the process of being healed to minister healing to hurting people around them. Underlying Nouwen's teaching is the idea that God uses both our strengths and our weaknesses for His glory. Our weaknesses should not withhold us from offering ourselves to God's purposes. This is an important lesson for leaders, especially in the Christian community, which often acts as if God uses only our strengths. Yes, God does use our strengths, but He is not limited to using them alone.

Because of the false idea that God can only use strong and talented people for His purposes, many Christians choose to give up their God-given leadership and remain inactive in God's work. This is a great loss.

The apostle Paul is a strong witness in support of the idea that God works through us in spite of our weaknesses. He talked about his own thorn in the flesh (2 Cor. 12:7). Whatever it was, one thing is clear: God told him that His grace was sufficient for him. The lesson Paul learned was that God's strength could be made perfect in his weakness. In other words, God reveals His strength through our weaknesses and accomplishes His purposes.

By "weakness," I do not mean constant moral failures. I am speaking of the inabilities and inadequacies that all of us experience in life. It may also mean a situational difficulty or some form of handicap.

Look at the history of God's people. Have you considered the unlikely people God has used? Abraham was too old. Moses was a stutterer. Timothy had stomach problems. Hosea had a terrible marriage. Amos was untrained. Thomas was a doubter. Peter was impulsive. The list can go on and on. But God used all these people in spite of their issues.

I remember the words of Dean Colin Williams at Yale Divinity School long ago. He stated that the degrees we were earning were only like the five loaves of bread in the hands of a lad. They could not feed the hungry crowd, but if we would give them to Jesus, He would bless them, break them, and multiply them to feed the multitude!

Please don't be discouraged because someone else has more skills and talents than you have. Give your strengths as well as your weaknesses to God and ask Him to use them for His glory. He will take them in His hands, break them, bless them, and use them for His purposes. What matters is your surrender to God. He will use your strengths, work thorough your brokenness, and make everything beautiful in His time.

Do not sabotage your destiny by nurturing and enlarging the perceptions of your weaknesses and catastrophizing bad experiences. Claim your strengths and your weaknesses. Give them to God. Let Him use your strengths and redeem your weaknesses. Be the leader God has destined you to be. Walk in the power of your identity as a Spirit-empowered leader, and fulfill your purpose.

Questions for Reflection

1. List some of the leaders in the Old and New Testaments. Feel free to add people not mentioned in this chapter.
2. Who are some of the leaders in the history of the church mentioned in this chapter? Add your personal selection of local and global leaders to this list.
3. What is Pastor Maldonado's definition of a ministry leader?
4. List the qualities and values you would add to Pastor Maldonado's list.
5. Give a personal definition of Spirit-empowered servant leadership.
6. What are the three characteristics of Spirit-empowered leadership described in this chapter?
7. Describe why you believe leadership development is a process by pointing out three key leaders God developed?
8. Comment on how God uses our strengths and weaknesses for His purposes.
9. Where is God working in your development as a leader?
10. What is He asking you to do regarding that area?

Chapter 9

One day Jesus said to his disciples, "Let us go over to the other side of the lake." So they got into a boat and set out.

—LUKE 8:22

The disciples of Jesus, in spite of their proximity to the Son of God, got mixed up on many important matters. For example, these healing ministers tried to stop blind Bartimaeus from receiving his healing (Mark 10:48). One day they tried to stop little children from coming to Jesus to be blessed (Mark 10:13). On another occasion, they tried to stop a man from preaching in the name of Jesus because he was not one of them (Luke 9:49)!

It appears that Peter got more mixed up than his colleagues did. Remember the time when Jesus spoke about His sacrificial death? Peter said no to the idea (Matt. 16:23). When Jesus wanted to wash his feet, again, Peter said no (John 13:8). When he was asked to visit the house of Cornelius the Gentile, Peter would have said no again; it took a great vision and other divine appointments to finally get Peter to cooperate with God's plans for Cornelius and his family (Acts 10:9ff).

We also get mixed up on spiritual matters. For example, we get mixed up about public worship. We attend worship services and forget that we are participants in praise and worship. Instead, we act as if we are just a part of the audience, failing to realize that there is only one in the audience at worship—Jesus. Similarly, we get mixed up about missions and missionaries. We think that missionaries are highly unusual people who go abroad to preach to strange people. Yes, there are cross-cultural missionaries who go to faraway places, but missionaries are not just the few who go overseas. The truth is that all Christians are missionaries. Yes, you are a missionary. All followers of Jesus are missionaries whether we ever leave our hometown or not.

Have you thought about this question? What is the gospel in one verse? The answer is John 3:16: "For God so loved the world that he gave his one and only Son, that whoever believes in him shall not perish but have eternal life." What is the gospel in one word? I would say it is the word *Come.* "Come and see," Jesus invited (John 1:39 KJV). Another one-word summary of the gospel is *Go.* "Let us go over to the other side of the lake," Jesus said (Luke 8:22). "And he must needs go through Samaria," we read later (John 4:4 KJV). "Let us go back to Judea," He told His disciples (John 11:7). And "Therefore go and make disciples of all nations, baptizing them in the name of the Father and of the Son and of the Holy Spirit," He commissioned (Matt. 28:19). The gospel has to do with coming to Jesus and going to others in His name.

Christians belong to a missionary family. God the Father is a missionary. God the Son is a missionary. God the Holy Spirit is a missionary. God's church is a missionary church. And every believer is a missionary, the Holy Spirit being the first missionary to all places. No human missionary is the first one to get anywhere with the good news; the Holy Spirit is the first witness. He gets to people and reaches out to them before we ever get there. Then you become a missionary.

The church is called the *ecclesia* in Greek. This word means the assembly of the ones who are called. We are called to come and go. This is not just for professional ministers to consider; it is every Christian's vocation. We are all called to go, locally and globally:

*   We must go with the presence of God.
*   We must go with the Word of God.
*   We must go with the power of God.

We must go with the presence of God. The presence of God is with us through the Holy Spirit. The apostle Paul tells us that Christ through His Spirit dwells in us (Col. 1:27). We must go with the awareness of the presence of His Spirit in us.

We must go with the word of God. God's Word is a word of salvation. God's word is a word of healing. God's word is a word of deliverance. God's word is a liberating word. It is a word of freedom.

Moses had to go with the word of God to confront the Pharaoh. He had to declare God's word and say, "Let my people go." Elijah had to go with the word of God and stand before Ahab. He said, "As the LORD, the God of Israel, lives, whom I serve, there will be neither dew nor rain in the next few years except at my word" (1 Kings 17:1). Jonah had to go with God's word and declare it in Nineveh. He had to share a call to repentance (Jon. 1:1; 3:4). Peter took the word of salvation to the house of Cornelius. Paul had to go to the Gentiles with God's word. We must also go with the word of God.

We must go with the power of God. God's Word must be delivered in power. Missionaries are not people who do freaky things to freak out people. Missionaries are people who move in the power of the Holy Spirit as they go with the presence of God and the Word of God in the power of the Holy Spirit.

Look what happened when Paul and Silas traveled with the word of God and the power of the Holy Spirit. They wound up in a prison in Philippi. In the middle of the night, they began to praise God as the other prisoners were listening to the strange new arrivals. The prison doors began to shake until they finally opened. The prisoners were shocked to see their chains falling. The jailer in charge got scared and tried to commit suicide, but he found salvation by faith in Jesus that night, along with his entire family. They were baptized by the apostles while it was still night. Their sins were washed away in the blood of Jesus. The reborn jailer was found washing the wounds of the missionaries that very night (Acts 16:33).

According to the book of Acts, we must go with the power of the name of Jesus (Acts 3:6). We must go in the power of the Holy Spirit (Acts 1:8). We must go in the power of holy living and in the power of holy giving (Acts 5:5).

Many Christians believe the lie that preachers and paid professionals are the only ones called to share the gospel. To make matters worse, many believe that public preaching is the only way to minister. These are lies of the enemy to keep the body of Christ inactive. The truth, as I've said throughout this chapter, is that we are all ministers and missionaries. Yes, every Christian is a missionary—even you.

I believe this because of the following facts.

* Fact: We live in a culture of entertainment, reverse values, violence, and materialism.
* Fact: People are hurting in body, mind, spirit, relationships, and finances. Even the environment—yes, the whole creation—is groaning (Rom. 8:22).
* Fact: From the majority world to the most advanced nations, there is a desperate need for hope in the world today.
* Fact: Our interconnected, globalized world has given us more isolation than ever before. What we have is virtual connectedness and real isolation!

* Fact: The isolated, lonely, high-tech world is hungry for a high-touch ministry. People are sick of selecting "from the following menu." They long for a human touch.
* Fact: Materialism and consumerism are not meeting the deepest needs of humanity. Unbridled borrowing and uncontrolled spending leave us only underwater mortgages and bankruptcies.
* Fact: Cutting-edge research and blockbuster pills have not given us whole-person healing.
* Fact: From board rooms of corporations where billion-dollar decisions are made to kitchen tables where decisions are made about personal medical procedures, people are looking for wise and ethical counsel. Someone must help them.
* Fact: Unethical business practices and greed-based financial dealings are leaving millions of wounded people fearful and hopeless from Wall Street to Main Street and far beyond our shores. Caught in the web of a global economy, they are looking for someone to offer a word of hope and promise.
* Fact: All have sinned and come short of the glory of God. But the gift of God is eternal life through our Lord Jesus Christ (Rom. 3:23 KJV; 6:23).
* Fact: The twenty-first century requires every believer to be a missionary by being a giver and a goer into his or her own world. We need to go and make disciples of all nations. We must go into all the world and to every person's world. We need to be global, local, and glocal Christians!

What is missions? Let me ease your anxiety by defining missions from a biblical perspective.

First, missions is being before doing. In missions we imitate God. Missions begins within our inner being. It is our "doing" flowing out of our "being."

Second, missions is being with Jesus. Incoming seminarians often respond to my question, "Why did Jesus ordain the twelve disciples?" by saying that they were ordained to preach, teach, and heal. They are surprised when I point out Mark 3:14–15: "He appointed twelve *that they might be with him* and that he might send them out to preach and to have authority to drive out demons" (emphasis added). Missions has to do with our being with Jesus first. Everything we do in missions must begin with that.

Third, missions is being like Jesus. Paul said, "Follow my example, as I follow the example of Christ" (1 Cor. 11:1). In other words, imitate me and be like me as I become like Christ. How do you become like Jesus? We look like Jesus when we love others. Being like Jesus means loving as Jesus did. You don't have to leave your country to love people. You don't have to leave your neighborhood to love others. You don't even have to leave your house to love others.

Fourth, missions is being an "incarnational presence" of Christ. It is being present with others in the name of Jesus Christ. Jesus was the word-become-flesh. Christ in us is the hope of glory (Col. 1: 27). Representing the presence of Jesus in our life and serving others no matter where we are is missions. God can use our words. He can also use wordless actions as missionary work.

Missions is ultimately hope-bearing. It is sharing hope with our hopeless world today. We share this hope by being engaged in the lives of those around us in the name of Jesus. Christ in us is hope (Col. 1:27).

Missions is being in dialogue. A true Christian is in dialogue with God and humans simultaneously. As all true dialogue requires listening, tuning in to people around us with a desire to share the hope we found in Jesus with them is missions.

In that sense, missions is hospitality. True hospitality involves making room for others in your heart. This is not for professional helpers only, nor is it just for the highest-trained ministers. This is for all followers of Jesus. We are called to open our hearts and be hospitable to a hurting world. And this is what makes all of us missionaries.

Why is this important?

* Because the children across the world are crying out. We must not stop them from coming to Jesus, as some of His disciples did.
* Because the sick and the needy are calling out like blind Bartimaeus. We should not rebuke them and tell them to be quiet.
* Because the hungry of the world are calling us. We should not just count the cost and be paralyzed.
* Because nations are asking us, like the Ethiopian eunuch, "Look, here is water, what hinders me from being baptized?" (Acts 8:36 NKJV). We should not just consider the inconvenience and ignore them.

* And because the Master is calling us. He is calling us to reach out and touch them. He is calling us to heal them and disciple them. He is asking us to give them something to eat.

Jesus is asking us, "Who will go for Us? Whom shall We send?" And how should we respond?
Will it be:

* "I cannot go because I have no time."
* "I cannot go because I have no money."
* "I cannot go because I have other obligations and ambitions."
* "I cannot go because I'm afraid."

Or will our answer be: "Here am I, Lord. Send me!"?

Aby was my student at Oral Roberts University many years ago. His father was a missionary in North India. One day he was distributing tracts to a Hindu crowd on the banks of the river Ganges. In the twilight of the evening, from a distance, he saw a man throwing something into the river. It looked like a baby, he thought. Hoping his perceptions were wrong, Aby's father ran to the man and realized that his worst thought was a reality. The man had thrown his baby into the river in obedience to the instructions of a local priest the day before. He had gone to the priest seeking peace. The priest told him that to find lasting peace, he had to sacrifice whatever was most precious to him. The man had two children, one healthier than the other. He had just thrown his healthy baby into the river. As the baby drowned and disappeared in the sacred river, the man's wife stood next to him, crying out and screaming. Absorbing their pain for a few moments, the missionary gently told them about Jesus, the prince of peace, and the supreme sacrifice he made on the cross of Calvary for them. He told them that no additional sacrifices were needed for real peace or salvation. To his utter conviction, the mother of the baby looked up and asked him in a bitter voice, "Where were you half an hour ago?"

We do not have a lot of time to waste or to wait for professionals to arrive with the news. Neither do we have time to make excuses. Jesus is asking us to launch out into the deep and let down our nets for a catch now. How will you and I respond?

Will it be, "I have just bought a field, and I must go and see it. Please excuse me" (Luke 14:18)?

Or, "I have just bought five yoke of oxen, and I'm on my way to try them out. Please excuse me" (Luke 14:19)?

Or, "I just got married, so I can't come" (Luke 14:20)?

Or will it be, "Master, we've worked hard all night and haven't caught anything. But because you say so, I will let down the nets" (Luke 5:5)?

Near or far does not matter, but will you go? Will you recognize that you are a missionary?

Yes, you are a missionary. Walk in the awareness of who you are. Walk in the power of the Holy Spirit. Be a Spirit-led missionary in your daily life regardless of what that life normally is.

Questions for Reflection

1. What were some of the issues the disciples of Jesus mishandled?
2. What are some of the areas of Christian life that modern disciples of Jesus misunderstand?
3. What are some of the misunderstandings modern Christians have about missions and missionaries?
4. What are the shortest versions of the gospel given in this chapter?
5. What is your definition of the gospel?
6. How are we advised to "go" in this chapter? Describe.
7. Review the seven definitions of missions.
8. Give some reasons why everyday Christians should see themselves as missionaries.
9. How should the church's missionary work look today?
10. What is your mission field? Reflect on your life as a missionary.

Chapter 10

▲ ▲ ▲

You Are a Prophet

"And afterward,
I will pour out my Spirit on all people.
Your sons and daughters will prophesy,
your old men will dream dreams,
your young men will see visions."

—*JOEL 2:28*

Prophecy is one of the most misunderstood ministries within the Christian community. In our age of the globalization of palm reading and psychic lines, many people seem to think that prophets are some kind of predictors or soothsayers. Prophets are not just predictors of future events; they are people who speak for God. They may speak about the past in review, evaluate the present, or reveal the future. And biblical prophets were not limited to speaking. Some acted in peculiar ways to turn people's attention to God (see Hosea 1:2–3).

Prophets were called "seers" in the Old Testament. There were schools of prophets in ancient Israel apparently training prophets. We read about true and false prophets operating among the people of God, not counting the prophets of other religions.

The Old Testament prophets can be divided into three groups: (1) those before the time of the kings; (2) prophets who served during the reigns of the kings; and (3) classical prophets, whose writings are in the Bible.

The first group included Abraham, Aaron, Miriam, Moses, and Deborah (Ex. 7:1; Deut. 18:18; 34:10). God Himself called Abraham a prophet (see Gen. 20:1–7). Miriam is described as a dancing prophetess (Ex. 15:20). Deborah was a prophetess, wife, and leader concurrently (Judg. 4:4). The story of the appointment of Moses as a prophet (in his own words) reveals what God had in mind for the life and ministry of a prophet.

The nations you will dispossess listen to those who practice sorcery or divination. But as for you, the LORD your God has not permitted you to do so. The LORD your God will raise up for you a prophet like me from among you, from your fellow Israelites. You must listen to him. For this is what you asked of the LORD your God at Horeb on the day of the assembly when you said, "Let us not hear the voice of the LORD our God nor see this great fire anymore, or we will die."

> The LORD said to me: "What they say is good. I will
> raise up for them a prophet like you from among their
> fellow Israelites, and I will put my words in his mouth.
> He will tell them everything I command him." (Deut.
> 18:14–18)

The prophet's job description is clear in the Bible. God puts His words in the prophet's mouth, and he is to tell everything God puts in his mouth to the people. Prophets are called to receive God's word and then to pass it on. They are not to add or take away anything from what they receive from God, but must hear God carefully and then faithfully share with the people what God said. Prophets are the oracles of God.

The second group of prophets included Samuel, who appointed and terminated Saul as king; Nathan, who confronted David regarding his sin; Elijah, Elisha, and Micaiah, who were active during the reign of Ahab; and others. These prophets anointed kings and advised them, but also felt empowered to rebuke them when needed. Who can forget Nathan's confrontation of David?

> "You are the [guilty] man! This is what the LORD, the
> God of Israel, says: 'I anointed you king over Israel, and I
> delivered you from the hand of Saul. I gave your master's
> house to you, and your master's wives into your arms. I
> gave you all Israel and Judah. And if all this had been
> too little, I would have given you even more. Why did
> you despise the word of the LORD by doing what is evil

in his eyes? You struck down Uriah the Hittite with the sword and took his wife to be your own. You killed him with the sword of the Ammonites. Now, therefore, the sword will never depart from your house, because you despised me and took the wife of Uriah the Hittite to be your own.'" (2 Sam. 12:7–10)

Prophets had to be true to God. They had to overcome their fears and confront evil. They modeled speaking truth to power. Severe punishment was the lot of false prophets. "But a prophet who presumes to speak in my name anything I have not commanded, or a prophet who speaks in the name of other gods, is to be put to death" (Deut. 18:20).

The classical prophets (third group) are the ones with their words recorded in the Bible, from Amos to Isaiah. They wept and blessed, but were also known to do shocking things to get their message across. Hosea is a good example. "When the LORD began to speak through Hosea, the LORD said to him, 'Go, marry a promiscuous woman and have children with her, for like an adulterous wife this land is guilty of unfaithfulness to the LORD.' So he married Gomer daughter of Diblaim, and she conceived and bore him a son" (Hos. 1:2–3).

According to scholars, the Old Testament prophets gave seven types of messages. First, they gave "Thus says the LORD" messages. These were direct words from the Lord.

The second type of messages reminded people of God's relationship with them. Here are examples:

Hear me, you heavens! Listen, earth! For the Lord has spoken: "I reared children and brought them up, but they have rebelled against me." (Isa. 1:2)

He tends his flock like a shepherd: He gathers the lambs in his arms and carries them close to his heart; he gently leads those that have young. (Isa. 40:11)

The word of the Lord came to me: "Go and proclaim in the hearing of Jerusalem: This is what the Lord says: 'I remember the devotion of your youth, how as a bride you loved me and followed me through the wilderness, through a land not sown.'" (Jer. 2:2).

The third type of messages revealed God's broken heart:

"My people have committed two sins: They have forsaken me, the spring of living water, and have dug their own cisterns, broken cisterns that cannot hold water." (Jer. 2:13)

"But the more they were called, the more they went away from me. They sacrificed to the Baals and they burned incense to images." (Hos. 11:2)

The fourth type was messages of God's judgment.

"I will punish him and his children and his attendants for their wickedness; I will bring on them and those living in Jerusalem and the people of Judah every disaster I pronounced against them, because they have not listened." (Jer. 36:31)

"They will not remain in the LORD's land; Ephraim will return to Egypt and eat unclean food in Assyria." (Hos. 9:3)

The next type of messages expressed God's mercy and compassion:

"How can I give you up, Ephraim? How can I hand you over, Israel? How can I treat you like Admah? How can I make you like Zeboyim? My heart is changed within me; all my compassion is aroused." (Hos. 11:8)

Go, proclaim this message toward the north: "'Return, faithless Israel,' declares the LORD, 'I will frown on you no longer, for I am faithful,' declares the LORD, 'I will not be angry forever.'" (Jer. 3:12)

The sixth type was God's message of redemption: "Those the LORD has rescued will return. They will enter Zion with singing; everlasting joy will crown their heads. Gladness and joy will overtake them, and sorrow and sighing will flee away" (Isa. 51:11).

Messages of hope and promise form the last type:

"I will also make you a light for the Gentiles, that my salvation may reach to the ends of the earth." (Isa. 49:6)

"In the last days the mountain of the LORD's temple will be established as the highest of the mountains; it will be exalted above the hills, and all nations will stream to it." (Isa. 2:2)

> For to us a child is born, to us a son is given, and the government will be on his shoulders. And he will be called Wonderful Counselor, Mighty God, Everlasting Father, Prince of Peace (Isa. 9:6).

Prophecy did not end with the Old Testament. Many under the new covenant prophesied. Zechariah (Luke 1:67), John the Baptist (Matt. 14:5; Luke 1:76), Simeon (Luke 2:25–26), and Anna (Luke 2:36) were considered prophets. Jesus was called a prophet (Matt. 16:13–14). Philip the deacon had four unmarried daughters who prophesied (Acts 21:9). There were prophets in Antioch and Ephesus (Acts 13:1; 19:6).

Prophecy is listed among the manifestations of the Holy Spirit. It is one of the gifts of the Holy Spirit. Paul encouraged the believers in Corinth to "follow the way of love and eagerly desire gifts of the Spirit, especially prophecy" (1 Cor. 14:1). He also gave the litmus test for authentic prophecy. It strengthens, encourages, and comforts (1 Cor. 14:3). Prophecy is not a tool in the hands of some to spook others. In the New Testament, if a prophecy does not produce strengthening, encouragement, and comfort, it remains suspect.

The world needs prophets today. There is a desperate need for prophetic voices in our day. It is hard to differentiate the voice of God in today's noise. We need people who can hear the voice of God in this noisy world and share it with clarity and conviction. There are spokespersons for all sorts of people and organizations in modern culture, but there is a real shortage of individuals to speak for God.

We can look back and recognize the prophetic voices of the past, but it is not easy to name truly prophetic voices today. Many voices that could be considered prophetic are drowning in their own issues of credibility. Many good voices are so aligned with the movements and organizations of the world outside the church that they are not taken seriously as God's representatives. Even when they have a word from the Lord, they are not considered to be speaking for God.

The church also needs prophets. We see a form of godliness in many places, but there is no power in demonstration. There is a party spirit within the church but not enough prayer. We have seminars on prayer, but not enough praying. There are many learning places, but there is no burning left in the students at the end of their learning. While Peter's anointed preaching on the day of Pentecost produced three thousand converts, thousands of our sermons are not producing many converts. We talk about healing, but do not pray for the sick. We have many large gatherings, but many of them leave no lasting impact. Giving in the church is way below the tithes of the people. We need prophets to awaken us.

Our priorities are mixed up. We emphasize external holiness and ignore the matters of the heart. We emphasize our organizations but forget that we are called to be a living organism. We have large budgets, but our faith is not matching. We have abundant formalities, but we lack in love. We testify within the church but are afraid to witness outside its walls. We emphasize either the need for education or the Spirit's anointing for our preachers, but not both. Women are asked to work hard in the church, but in many places they are marginalized and not allowed to minister. We need prophets.

Biblical prophets did much more than talk. They assisted people in their struggles, like Elijah, who helped the Zarephath woman (1 Kings 17:10ff). Elisha helped the widow of the indebted prophet whose sons were about to be enslaved (2 Kings 4:1ff).

Prophets have been healers. Some healings can be called prophetic healing. We know that there are many ways to heal people. For instance, confession of sins has healing power (James 5:16). The apostles' shadow caused people to be healed (Acts 5:15). Handkerchiefs and aprons that had touched Paul served as points of contact for healing (Acts 19:12). Casting out demons produced healing (Matt. 8:28–34). Word of knowledge resulted in healing. Examples are plenty: "Your faith has healed you" (Matt. 9:22). "Pick up your mat and walk" (John 5:8). "Your sins are forgiven" (Mark 2:9). "Silver or gold I do not have, but what I do have I give you. In the name of Jesus Christ of Nazareth, walk" (Acts 3:6). God sends forth his word and heals (Ps. 107:20). Healing is a ministry of the word of God. It is a prophetic ministry. Prophets have ministered healing to individuals and communities, like Elisha, who ministered healing to Naaman (2 Kings 5:10) and purified the water that was killing the land (2 Kings 2:21). We need prophets today.

I do not wish to give the wrong impression that prophets have to be great, charismatic personalities. It is true that we had great prophetic personalities in the Bible and since then, but I am convinced that something significant has changed in this regard since the day of Pentecost. I don't believe prophets have to be great, outgoing personalities anymore. Neither do I believe that they have to write their prophecies in book form. Let me tell you what I believe a prophet looks like now.

The answer begins in the book of Joel. His prophecy regarding the last days contains the secret. Age is not a factor in the selection of a current prophet. "And afterward, I will pour out my Spirit on all people. Your sons and daughters will prophesy, your old men will dream dreams, your young men will see visions. Even on my servants, both men and women, I will pour out my Spirit in those days" (Joel 2:28–29). Age, gender, social status, and occupation are irrelevant to one's service as a prophet. God has demonstrated that He can use some very ordinary people for his extraordinary purposes. William Seymour was an African American from the American South before the civil rights movement. He was a man with only one healthy eye. God used him to lead the great Azusa Street revival, which became the central point of the modern Spirit-empowered movement. Aimee Semple McPherson was a widow whom God used to establish the International Church of the Foursquare Gospel. Kathryn Kuhlman was a very ordinary woman who was used to minister healing to multitudes of people. Oral Roberts was a man with a Native American heritage who came from a Pentecostal Holiness preacher's home in Oklahoma.

According to Joel, our sons and daughters can prophesy. I don't know how Christians can hold their daughters back from speaking for God in their generation. Who else will share God's Word with half a billion Muslim women who will have nothing to do with a male member of any race? How can we forget that Jesus gave the message of His resurrection first to a woman? Mary was the one entrusted with that message. She was asked to give it to Peter. What has happened to us?

In the careful recording of the events of the day of Pentecost, we do not see the demographics including gender. Three thousand were added to the church that day. Their nationalities and diversity of languages are mentioned. Gender is not. Listen to Paul: "There is neither Jew nor Gentile, neither slave nor free, nor is there male and female, for you are all one in Christ Jesus" (Gal. 3:28). We should not try to outsmart the apostle Paul in this matter. I believe the church has to stop saying we must keep both Martha and Mary in the kitchen.

The issue is not gender; it is the infilling of the Holy Spirit and one's willingness to allow the gifts of the Spirit to flow through his or her life. Prophecy is a manifestation of the Spirit. Prophets can speak their mother tongues. They can use their own vernaculars. No one has to speak King James English to be a prophet in the twenty-first century.

What does a prophet look like? I am trying to say that a prophet looks like you, if you have received the Holy Spirit. A prophet looks like you if you love Jesus. A prophet looks like you if you have compassion for people. A prophet looks like you if you can hear the voice of God in this noisy world. A prophet looks like you if you are willing to share the Word of God with humility and power. A prophet looks like you if you are compelled in your spirit to encourage, strengthen, and comfort others. A prophet looks like you if you are willing to depend on the Holy Spirit to live a sanctified life in this unholy world.

The Holy Spirit has given you the capacity to speak for God. Your audience may be large or small. It does not matter. You are called to speak God's message to your generation. It may be through preaching, teaching, exhorting, strengthening, or comforting. Simply be obedient. As a Spirit-empowered person, you are a prophet. Speak to your community. Speak to your nation and call it back to God. Declare God's healing to the nations. Walk in your calling as a prophet in the power of the Holy Spirit.

Questions for Reflection

1. Name several prophets in the Old and New Testaments.
2. List the three groups of prophets in the Old Testament.
3. What were the seven types of prophetic messages in the Old Testament?
4. Why does the world need prophets today?
5. Why does the church need prophets?
6. What does Joel's prophecy say about the last days regarding prophecy?
7. What was the impact of the day of Pentecost on the ministry of prophecy?
8. Based on 1 Corinthians 14:3, what are the purposes of prophecy (Paul's litmus test)?
9. In your view, based on the New Testament, what does a modern-day prophet look like?
10. Can you discern a word from the Lord for this generation?

Part 3

Discover Your Power in God's Spirit

Chapter 11

▲ ▲ ▲

You Are a Temple, Not the Taj Mahal

Do you not know that your bodies are temples of the Holy Spirit, who is in you, whom you have received from God? You are not your own.

—1 CORINTHIANS 6:19

The Taj Mahal in Agra, India, is the most beautiful building I have ever seen. I have heard about it all my life, but did not expect it to be as big or beautiful as I saw it. Made of pure white marble and built by twenty thousand workers between 1632 and 1653, the Taj Mahal is the legacy of Muslim rulers of India who invaded the land in the seventeenth century.

Built in symmetry and reflecting in multiple pools, the Taj has a dome 120 feet tall and 70 feet in diameter. Four towers in each corner, called *minarets*, are 133 feet tall. The jewels complementing the marble are all gone now, plundered by thieves and colonists, but the white beauty still stands, with other materials replacing the stolen precious jewels. There is nothing like it in the world when the sunlit Taj reflects her beauty in the surrounding pools.

Passages from the Koran, the holy book of Islam, decorate the outside of the Taj, giving it the look of a place of worship. Tourists from all over the world stand in line to get a glimpse of the inside of this amazing structure. Security is tight. Cameras are controlled. Shoes must be left outside to get inside the building. It looks like a holy place, a temple.

But the Taj Mahal is not a temple; it is a tomb! Emperor Shah Jahan built it in memory of his beloved wife, Mumtaz, who died in childbirth. The emperor who loved her very much could not contain his sorrow, and he wanted to build a beautiful structure in her memory and honor that had no parallel in the world. He wanted the world forever to remember his beloved Mumtaz and his everlasting love for her.

So today the Taj Mahal remains a tomb, a memorial. It is a place of death, a place of memorialized pain and sorrow. It is not a temple.

The words of the apostle Paul come to mind: "Do you not know that your bodies are temples of the Holy Spirit, who is in you, whom you have received from God?" (1 Cor. 6: 19).

Paul was writing to the believers in Corinth, the fourth city in the Roman Empire. After Rome, Alexandria, and Ephesus, Corinth stood in line as a center of power and fame within the empire. It had the reputation of being an international city with cultural and commercial importance and much affluence. People from Egypt, Syria, Italy, Israel, and the Orient had migrated there. In fact, archaeologists have discovered Egyptian, Syrian, and Ephesian idols in Corinth's ruins.

Corinth had a certain reputation in the ancient world. It was well known for alcoholism, immorality, materialism, divorce, and dysfunctional families. It was a modern city where important things were happening. The citizens were proud of their city, but deeply mired in its social, cultural, and political decay.

There was a vibrant church in Corinth. It included both Jewish and Gentile members, both free and slaves. While most of the members were common people, the congregation included some people of noble birth. Some members were rich and powerful and considered themselves wise. One high-powered member was Erastus, the city treasurer.

Men and women were actively involved in the life of the Corinthian church. It appears that the church met in homes or rented public places. Scholars estimate the size of the congregation to be between 40 to 150 people. It was a charismatic church, but there were some real problems in this church that had deep apostolic connections.

There were divisions within the church. Members were suing one another. They argued about food served to idols. They conducted disorderly communion services and poor fellowship gatherings. Some ate too much; others drank excessively. The list of problems is long: pagan holidays, wild parties, idolatry, immorality, and false teachings. Some did not believe in the resurrection of the dead. Others taught that human knowledge is sufficient for salvation. Some puffed-up members encouraged others to eat, drink, and be merry!

It is hard to believe that a church founded by the apostle Paul was in this condition. Paul had spent eighteen months in this city beginning in AD 51 or 52, planting this church. Things have changed. It is clear that the root of these problems stemmed from the influence of the secular Corinthian culture on this multicultural church.

Obviously, church members ate with nonbelievers. We know that outsiders visited this church and observed its practices. We are not sure how it happened, but it is very clear that the church began to look like mainstream Corinth. It looks as though the Christianization of the pagans paganized the church.

To these believers who lost their way and conformed to their culture Paul said three things:

1) You are not your own.
2) You have been bought at a price.
3) Your body is the temple of the Holy Spirit.

Paul was calling their attention to their true identity.

Does Corinth look familiar to you? No wonder. Even Tulsa, Oklahoma, known as the buckle of the Bible belt, home to the ministries of T. L. Osborn, Oral Roberts, and Kenneth Hagin, where I have lived for more than three decades, looks very much like Corinth.

Look at our own day. Consider our own way. Can't you see the parallel? Take a look at our own culture and its influence on the church.

We live in a culture of entertainment. It is hard to tell the difference between edification and entertainment now. Technology has brought us infinite ways of entertaining ourselves.

We have a culture of reverse values. Indecent has become decent. Modesty is mocked. Apostles and prophets are marginalized. Lawbreakers and immoral celebrities have the center stage of culture.

We live in a culture of disbelief and violence. We don't trust pastors or journalists anymore. We lock up juries and free criminals. Atheism is fashionable. Violence is glorified in video games, but it threatens our very existence. Abortion is a "procedure." Murder is being called mercy killing. The culture just changed its vocabulary to accommodate the new thinking.

Ours is a culture of human-centered materialism. Things are more important than people in our culture. Ownership is more important than relationships.

Let's face it: we are the new Corinthian Christians. We are deeply influenced by our culture, and we keep adjusting ourselves like the proverbial frog in the kettle. We are in denial, but we are conforming to this world.

The result is powerless living, having a form of godliness without the power (2 Tim. 3:5). Paul's words apply to us. We must take them to heart. We must confront our conformity. We must discover our true identity.

We are not our own. We have been bought with the precious blood of Jesus. Hollywood did not pay the price. Wall Street did not pay the price. Washington did not pay the price. God in Jesus did. He did it in a historically unique way, once and for all. God became man for us. The Creator became creation for us. The Infinite became an infant for us. The Word became flesh for us.

Paul was speaking of Jesus of Nazareth, the Son of the living God. Jesus, Emmanuel, God with us. He became obedient unto death for us. The sinless One became sin for us. We are not our own. We are not our own to worry about, work for, or worship.

Our brains are not our own. Our degrees are not our own. All that we are and all that we own belong to God. This is radical.

We must glorify God with our bodies and spirits. Remember that 1 Corinthians was penned at a time when Greek philosophy separated body and spirit. Only the spirit had to deal with God. The body was for one's own pleasure. Concerning the body, the advice was, "Eat, drink, and be merry!" (see Luke 12:13–20). Paul disagreed. We must glorify God with body and spirit, he said. Considering his words to the Thessalonians, we may say that we are required to glorify God with our bodies, minds, and spirits (1 Thess. 5:23).

We must submit our bodies to God as a living sacrifice. Our bodies are an offering to God. Our minds are to be renewed by the power of the Spirit of God to bring glory to God. This means that even for hard sciences, the ultimate purpose must be to discover the glory of God. Our spirits are to commune with the Spirit of God. Our work, worship, rest, and play must glorify God.[23]

In a culture that was advising its citizens to glorify the self, the apostle advised the Corinthian believers to glorify God. The purpose of life is not eating, drinking, and being merry; it is glorifying God.

Your body is the temple of the Holy Spirit. Here's our true identity. Here is the source of our true power. This is the secret of the power of powerlessness.

The Old Testament talks about three temples: Solomon's original temple, Zerubbabel's rebuilt temple, and Herod's updated temple. The New Testament talks about two temples: The church of Jesus Christ as the temple of God, and the believers' physical bodies as temples of the Holy Spirit. This is a profound truth: our bodies are temples of the Holy Spirit.

The Taj Mahal is not a temple. It is a tomb. It is beautiful on the outside, but it contains the remains of a dead queen. The difference between a temple and a tomb is LIFE. Are you a temple or a Taj Mahal?

A temple is a beautiful place. It is interesting to note that Paul did not say that your body is the tabernacle of the Holy Spirit. That would have been fine, as the tabernacle represented the presence of God with His people. It was the dwelling place of God that accompanied them throughout their desert journey. Its inside was truly beautiful, but the outside had a "covering of ram skins dyed red, and over that a covering of hides of sea cows"

---

23 The idea of life as work, worship, rest, and play is from Richard Exley's book *The Rhythm of Life : Putting Life's Priorities in Perspective* (n.p.: Honor, 1987).

(Ex. 26:14). It is hard to imagine that this was visually most beautiful. Solomon's temple, on the other hand, had the most grand and beautiful interior and exterior. The interior walls were covered with cedar wainscoting, and the floor was covered with boards of cypress, overlaid with pure gold. Solomon's wealth and majesty were in display throughout the temple in honor of Yahweh. Gold work and artistry in bronze were prominent in the temple. Gold was lavishly used in the temple, as everything was trimmed with gold. Look at the description of the huge portico at the front:

> The portico at the front of the temple was twenty cubits long across the width of the building and twenty cubits high. He overlaid the inside with pure gold. He paneled the main hall with juniper and covered it with fine gold and decorated it with palm tree and chain designs. He adorned the temple with precious stones. And the gold he used was gold of Parvaim. He overlaid the ceiling beams, doorframes, walls and doors of the temple with gold, and he carved cherubim on the walls. (2 Chron. 3:4–7)

The inside of the Holy of Holies was overlaid "with six hundred talents [twenty-three tons] of fine gold (2 Chron. 3:8)!

The temple was simply beautiful inside and out. There is an important lesson in this that we should consider.

Many Christians live with a very poor self-concept. In our over-sensualized culture, many women, particularly younger ones, see themselves as ugly or at least unattractive. This makes room for discouragement and sometimes for depression. This also leads many to unhealthy ways of dealing with their poor self-concept, sometimes overcompensating for their false sense of beauty in detrimental ways. The enemy uses this opening to create more chaos in these lives. You are the temple of the Holy Spirit. You are beautifully and wonderfully created. God is your Designer and Maker. He has created you in His own image. He sees you as beautiful as can be. As the temple of the Holy Spirit, you are simply beautiful inside and out. Accept God's design. See what He sees in you. He calls you beautiful.

A temple is a place of prayer. It is a consecrated place. "My house shall be called a house of prayer," Jesus said (Mark 11:17 NKJV).

Have you thought about this? The difference between a social worker and a Christian social worker is prayer. The difference between a teacher and a Christian teacher is prayer. What distinguishes a psychologist, a businessperson, or a nurse from his or her secular counterpart is prayer.

Your body is the temple of the Holy Spirit. A temple is a place of prayer. You are a person of prayer. Prayer here is a reference to praying without ceasing (1 Thess. 5:17). It is not just about formal prayers or set times of prayer. It is about a lifestyle of prayer. It is about being in constant contact with God without ceasing. As the space shuttle was in constant contact with mission control during its flights, a believer is in regular contact with the Lord. A Christian is in dialogue with God on an ongoing basis. It may not look like a religious act. It is a relational matter. It is an attempt to hear the voice of God. It is a way to listen to God's direction at crucial times. It is a way of living, a way of being. It has to do with one's identity.

This prayer is not an act of anxiety. It is not a restless ritual. It is an expression of confidence in God. It is an acknowledgment of who you are and whom you serve.

I had the strange idea one day to count the number of words in the Lord's Prayer. I found that the prayer in the King James Version had sixty-six words, and the New International Version's rendering contained fifty-two words. That's when I felt led to notice that there were only seven words about my personal needs in that prayer: "Give us this day our daily bread" (Matt. 6:11 KJV). It is about 10 percent of the Lord's Prayer. I learned a lesson that day. My needs should not be the majority of my prayer requests. I was convicted that day and have tried to be mindful of that in my prayer life ever since, unfortunately not always successfully. My prayers must glorify God, seek His kingdom, request forgiveness, present my needs, and look for deliverance.

I think of the prodigal son's prayer and how it changed. Before he left home, his prayer was all about receiving from the father. He said, "Give me . . ." (Luke 15:12). However, when he repented and returned, he had a different prayer. It was not about receiving. It was not about his rights. He prayed, "Make me . . ." (v. 19). There are "give me" prayers and "make me" prayers. Since our good Father already knows what we need, we must balance our "give me" prayers with some "make me" prayers. The "make me" prayers have to do with change and transformation. Amazingly, the prodigal son received more than all he could ask or think from his father even as he prayed "Make me . . ."

A temple is a place of power. Your body is the temple of the Holy Spirit. A temple is a place where God's power is expected to manifest. Therefore, you are a person of spiritual power. Walk in the power of the Holy Spirit. I am amazed at the number of Christians who are afraid of the devil. We must take the devil seriously, as Jesus did, because he is evil, but we should not be afraid of him. Remember the words of the apostle, "The one who is in you is greater than the one who is in the world" (1 John 4:4).

Matthew tells us that the blind and the lame came into the temple when Jesus was there. Many of them did not leave the temple blind and lame. God's power manifested in the temple through the hands of Jesus and healed them. Jesus was full of the Holy Spirit, we are told (Luke 4:1), and he had the power to heal the sick. He opened blind eyes and deaf ears. He raised the dead and set the captives free. The fact that your body is the temple of the Holy Spirit means that the same Spirit dwells in you, giving you access to the same power, with the potential to do even greater works than Jesus did (John 14:12). The apostle Paul said a great amen to this truth when he wrote, "And if the Spirit of him who raised Jesus from the dead is living in you, he who raised Christ from the dead will also give life to your mortal bodies because of his Spirit who lives in you" (Rom. 8:11). How amazing!

This does not make us arrogant, but it gives us confidence that we are more than conquerors through Christ (Rom. 8:37).

All things are possible through them that believe. We do not have to live in fear and anxiety. We do not have to feel intimidated by life or by bullies. Our bodies are the temples of the Holy Spirit. Take a moment to breathe this truth in. Take a moment to let this sink into your soul. Become aware of this truth at a deeper level of your being. You are a temple, not a Taj Mahal. Let this become a part of your identity at the deepest level, and learn to walk in this truth.

A temple is a place of worship. Your body is the temple of the Holy Spirit. A temple is a place of praise and worship. You are a worshipper. Abel was a worshipper. He could not be silenced even after his death (Heb. 11:4). Abraham, Isaac, and Jacob were worshippers. Each of them built altars to give God praise. Moses, Samuel, and David were worshippers. Have you read the description of the dedication of Solomon's temple? As they were worshipping God with gratitude and praise, the glory of God, the Shekinah, descended on them, and the priests could not minister (2 Chron. 5:13–14). Where there is the presence of God, there is worship. Where there is the praise of God, there is Shekinah.

For whatever reason, if you feel like a Taj Mahal even as you read these words, I have good news for you. God is in the business of turning tombs into temples. He can make a temple out of the Taj Mahal. Remember Lazarus, in John 11? He was in a tomb for four days. Things did not look good at all. His sisters were in grief. They had no reason to hope for anything before the final resurrection of the dead. But then came Jesus. He came to their house in Bethany and went on to the tomb where Lazarus was buried. John gives us the details. "Take away the stone," Jesus commanded, and then called out Lazarus by his name. Lazarus came alive and stood up. He was untied. Instantly, the tomb in Bethany became a temple. The crowd watched the whole thing in amazement. Jesus Christ is the same yesterday, today, and forever (Heb. 13:8). He can bring life to you and turn your sorrow into joy. He can make a temple out of your life today. Call on Him NOW. Open your life to Him and begin to walk in the newness of that life.

Remember: your body is the temple of the Holy Spirit. You are a temple, not a Taj Mahal, forever. This is your identity. Begin to walk in power and join the worship. Celebrate!

Questions for Reflection

1. What was the cultural situation in Corinth during Paul's time?
2. Do you agree with the analysis of our current culture in this chapter?
3. Do you have additional thoughts about the condition of the current culture?
4. How would you compare the Corinthian church with the twenty-first-century church?
5. How is today's church similar to or different from the Corinthian church?
6. What are the three major points Paul made in 1 Corinthians 6:19–20?
7. What are the four characteristics of a temple highlighted in this chapter?
8. Which of these characteristics speaks to you personally?
9. What is the Lord saying to you about this?
10. What resolution(s) would you make based on this particular issue or the whole chapter?

Chapter 12

▲ ▲ ▲

You Are a Gifted Person

*Peter replied, "Repent and be baptized,
every one of you, in the name of Jesus Christ
for the forgiveness of your sins. And you
will receive the gift of the Holy Spirit."*

—ACTS 2:38

Most Christians do not think of themselves as gifted people. In fact, many think of themselves in the opposite way. The truth is that all Spirit-filled Christians are gifted because the Holy Spirit is *the* gift. Listen to the words of the apostle Peter on the day of Pentecost: "Repent and be baptized, every one of you, in the name of Jesus Christ for the forgiveness of your sins. And you will receive the gift of the Holy Spirit" (Acts 2:38). Peter was not talking about the gifts or the manifestations of the Spirit as Paul described them in 1 Corinthians 12. Luke, the writer of Acts, made this clear in his account of the family of Cornelius: "While Peter was still speaking these words, the Holy Spirit came on all who heard the message. The circumcised believers who had come with Peter were astonished that the gift of the Holy Spirit had been poured out even on Gentiles" (Acts 10:44–45). To Peter, the Holy Spirit was *the* gift. This makes every Spirit-filled believer a gifted person.

What does it mean to be gifted with the Holy Spirit? We must take a closer look at the person and work of the Holy Spirit to answer this question.

We encounter the Holy Spirit as *Ruach* ("breath" in Hebrew) in the Old Testament. We meet Him as *Pneuma* ("Spirit" in Greek) in the New Testament. The Holy Spirit is often mistakenly referred to as an *it*. This is completely inappropriate, because the Holy Spirit is a person. We learn this first from Jesus: "But when he, the Spirit of truth, comes, he will guide you into all the truth. He will not speak on his own; he will speak only what he hears, and he will tell you what is yet to come" (John 16:13). This person has feelings, according to Paul; he can be grieved (Eph. 4:30). He speaks and teaches (Acts 2:4; 8:29). Jesus said, "But the Advocate, the Holy Spirit, whom the Father will send in my name, will teach you all things and will remind you of everything I have said to you" (John 14:26).

The Holy Spirit is symbolized in multiple ways in the Bible. These include water (Isa. 44:3), rivers (John 7:39), fire (Matt. 3:11; Acts 2:3), wind (Acts 2:2), a dove (Matt. 3:16), oil (Acts 10:38; 1 John 2:20–27), and wine (Acts 2:13–17; Eph. 5:18).

The Holy Spirit is known by different names. *Paraclete*, or Advocate (John 14:26), the Holy Spirit (Luke 11:13), the Spirit of truth (John 14:17), the Holy Spirit of promise (Eph. 1:13 NKJV), and the Spirit of glory and of God (1 Peter 4:14) are some of these names.

The Holy Spirit is visible and active both in the Old Testament and the New Testament. He was active in creation (Gen. 1:2). He was involved in the history of the people of God. For instance, the Egyptian Pharaoh noticed the "spirit of God" in Joseph (Gen. 41:38). Additionally, the Holy Spirit came on several people in the Old Testament. The list is long: Balaam (Num. 24:2), Gideon (Judg. 6:34), Samson (Judg. 14:6), Jephthah (Judg. 11:29), King Saul (1 Sam. 11:6), and prophets such as Zechariah (2 Chron. 24:20) and Ezekiel (Eze. 11:5). (We also read in the Old Testament about the Holy Spirit departing from Saul [1 Sam. 16:14].) The Holy Spirit came on individuals in the Old Testament to enable and equip them to perform certain tasks beyond their natural abilities. For instance, the superior knowledge and craftsmanship of Bezalel, who was involved in the building of the tabernacle, was attributed to the Spirit of God in him. Listen to the testimony of Moses regarding Bezalel, "See, the LORD has chosen Bezalel son of Uri, the son of Hur, of the tribe of Judah, and he has filled him with the Spirit of God, with wisdom, with understanding, with knowledge and with all kinds of skills—to make artistic designs for work in gold, silver and bronze, to cut and set stones, to work in wood and to engage in all kinds of artistic crafts" (Ex. 35:30–33). The Old Testament foresaw an outpouring of the Spirit on all flesh in the last days (Joel 2:28).

When we examine the New Testament, we see that the Holy Spirit was very active in the life of Jesus. Jesus was conceived by the Spirit (Matt. 1:20). The Spirit descended on Him like a dove at the time of His baptism (Matt. 3:16). The Spirit was present at His temptation in the wilderness and throughout His ministry (Luke 4:1, 14), manifesting His power in signs, wonders, and miracles (Matt. 12:28). Peter testified that the Spirit was present at the resurrection of Jesus (1 Peter 3:18).

Outside the life and ministry of Jesus, the Holy Spirit is very active and visible in the New Testament. The Gospel writers and Paul bear witness to the person and work of the Holy Spirit. John tells us that we are born of the Spirit. According to John, the Spirit of God is living water and a spring of water welling up within us (John 4:14; 7:38–39). He is also the breath of life; Jesus breathed on His disciples, saying to them, "Receive the Holy Spirit" (John 20:22).

The book of John presents us the most comprehensive teaching on the Holy Spirit given by Jesus. John reported that the Spirit will be given to us (14:16); will teach us (14:26); will convict the world of sin (16:8 KJV); and will show us things yet to come (16:12–14). Luke adds that the Holy Spirit will bear witness to Christ (Luke 12:11–12).

Luke, the author of both the gospel of Luke and the book of Acts, added a particular view of the Holy Spirit. We may say that Luke was a Pentecostal/charismatic historian. He provided us a unique angle to view the Holy Spirit. It is distinctive from even Paul's presentation of the Holy Spirit. According to Luke, Jesus is the one who baptizes us with the Holy Spirit and fire (Luke 3:16).

In Luke's writings, the Spirit comes in power; the Spirit can be seen, heard and perceived. One can be filled with the Spirit and be full of the Spirit. The Spirit belongs not only to us, but also to people in many generations to come. The Spirit can fall on (come on) us (Acts 11:15) and fill us (Luke 1:41; 1:67; Acts 2:4; 4:8; 4:31; 9:17; 13:9; 13:52). He can also be poured out on us (Acts 2:33; 10:45).

Luke presents a list of people in Acts who were filled with the Spirit. The 120 in the Upper Room belong to this group (Acts 2:4). Paul was also filled with the Spirit (Acts 9:17; 13:9). The family of Cornelius the Gentile received the Holy Spirit. Here is the story as Luke tells it:

> While Peter was still speaking these words, the Holy Spirit came on all who heard the message. The circumcised believers who had come with Peter were astonished that the gift of the Holy Spirit had been poured out even on Gentiles. For they heard them speaking in tongues and praising God. Then Peter said, "Surely no one can stand in the way of their being baptized with water. They have received the Holy Spirit just as we have." (Acts 10:44–47)

The followers of Jesus in Ephesus were also filled with the Spirit. We are told that "when Paul placed his hands on them, the Holy Spirit came on them, and they spoke in tongues and prophesied" (Acts 19:6).

It is easy to distinguish the people who are filled with the Spirit. According to Luke, they speak in tongues (Acts 2:4;

10:46; 19:6). They preach with boldness (Acts 2:11; 4:8, 31). They see visions and dreams, and they prophesy (Acts 11:12, 28; 20:23).

Luke has another list of people who are described as being full of the Holy Spirit. Jesus was full of the Holy Spirit (Luke 4:1). The early church deacons were full of the Holy Spirit (Acts 6:3). Stephen and Barnabas were full of the Holy Spirit (Acts 6:5; 11:24). So, according to Luke, the Holy Spirit can come on, or fall on, people and fill them. And individuals can remain full of the Holy Spirit.

The people who are (or remain) full of the Spirit seem to be those of very high character. They are active in ministry and occupy important leadership positions. We may conclude that being full of the Spirit must be a measure of their sanctification and indicate the level of the fruits of the Spirit in their lives.

The apostle Paul spent considerable time writing about the Holy Spirit and provided us a different perspective. There is only one Spirit, he said (Eph. 4:4), and he wanted all believers to be filled with that Spirit (Eph. 5:18). Paul presented the most well-known aspects of the Holy Spirit, namely, the gifts and fruits of the Spirit. In 1 Corinthians, Paul listed the nine gifts, literally manifestations, of the Spirit (8–10 KJV):

1. the word of wisdom
2. the word of knowledge
3. faith
4. gifts of healings
5. the working of miracles

6. prophecy
7. discerning of spirits
8. tongues
9. interpretation of tongues

Actually, this is only a partial list of the gifts of the Holy Spirit in Paul's writings. A more comprehensive list of the gifts of the Holy Spirit will include the following from Ephesians 4, Romans 12, and 1 Corinthians 12:

* apostles
* prophets
* evangelists
* pastor/teachers
* ministry
* teaching
* exhorting
* giving
* administration
* showing mercy
* celibacy

Two unusual experiences I had during my service at Oral Roberts University have made me realize the importance of the gifts of the Holy Spirit and His guidance in our lives. The first incident took place when I was the dean of students in the seminary. One day I had an impression in my spirit to check on a student. I tried to ignore it, but the concern did not leave, so I asked several professors and staff if they had seen this female student. Learning that no one had seen her, my concern increased. I decided to call the director of the graduate housing department. She also had not seen this seminarian for several days. I asked the director if I could join her to check the student's apartment. We were at the apartment door within minutes. The director used her master key to open the door. We could not believe what we saw! We found the young woman on the floor, fully unconscious. The director dialed 911 and within minutes the student was in an ambulance on the way to a nearby hospital. We learned that the student was in a diabetic coma and she would have died had we not discovered her. Thankfully, she did recover. It has been many years since this happened, but I never lost sight of the fact that this whole episode began with an impression in my spirit.

The second incident happened on an American Airlines flight from Dallas to Tulsa. I was returning from a speaking engagement in Palm Springs and settling down in my seat on my connecting flight in Dallas, eager to get home on a Sunday night. The short flight was scheduled to arrive in Tulsa by 10 p.m. A young lady who looked somewhat distressed took the seat next to me and started a conversation. Basically, she was telling me a story. She was a student at the University of Oklahoma and had her specific plans for her future, but recently felt called to earn a master's degree in counseling and enter a counseling ministry. She felt impressed to enroll in the MA in Christian Counseling degree program at

Oral Roberts University. This would be a big change in plans for her, and finances were a concern such that she said she needed a real confirmation of her impression. She had gone to visit her friends in the Northeast to discuss this change of plans, hoping they would provide her the confirmation she needed, but she was now on her way home without having received her friend's full affirmation. She mentioned that she had told the Lord if she did not receive a reliable confirmation before 10 p.m. that day, she would forget the idea of attending Oral Roberts University to become a counselor. I was intrigued and amused by her story, but kept listening to her without saying anything about my position at ORU. I noticed that the distress on her face was increasing as we began our descent to the Tulsa area. As we approached the runway just a few moments before 10 p.m., I told the young lady that I was the dean of the graduate school where the MA in Christian Counseling degree was housed, and if she enrolled, I would look for some extra scholarship for her. I will never forget her shock. Her jaw dropped and she sat like a tableau for a few moments. Soon the tears started flowing. She had received the confirmation she was seeking! I am glad to report that she did enroll at ORU, studied counseling, and became a counselor. I have asked her to speak to several incoming classes of students since then regarding the need to be guided by the Holy Spirit into their calling. This is another experience that taught me the importance of discernment and spiritual guidance.

In Galatians 5, Paul presented a list of nine fruits of the Spirit (vv. 22–23), in addition to his list of the gifts of the Spirit in 1 Corinthians. They are:

1. love
2. joy
3. peace
4. forbearance (KJV, longsuffering)
5. kindness (KJV, gentleness)
6. goodness
7. faithfulness (KJV, faith)
8. gentleness (KJV, meekness)
9. self-control (KJV, temperance)

Oral Roberts taught that these can be divided into three groups. The first three (love, joy, peace) minister to us. The second group (forbearance/longsuffering, kindness/gentleness, goodness) ministers to others. The last group (faithfulness/faith, gentleness/meekness, self-control/temperance) ministers to God. Faith pleases God (Heb. 11:6). Gentleness (meekness) and self-control (temperance) bring glory to God.

It is clear that the gifts (as manifestations) of the Spirit will operate in us and through us, but the fruits of the Spirit must be cultivated by us as they help us to grow in Christlikeness. The Holy Spirit works in us to make us holy and sanctified. We must receive the Spirit and be filled with the Spirit. We must seek to be (remain) full of the Spirit. That means we must open our lives to the coming (outpouring) and working of the Holy Spirit in us for our empowerment and sanctification. We are encouraged to desire the gifts of the Spirit (1 Cor. 14:1), and it is natural to seek them for empowerment, but our need for the sanctifying work of the Spirit within us is vital, according to Paul. We need both the gifts and the fruits of the Spirit in our lives.

The impact of the coming of the Spirit on the day of Pentecost is described in Acts. The following things happened after the Spirit came:

* The church grew (2:41, 47).
* Those who received the Spirit enjoyed great fellowship (2:42).
* There were signs and wonders (2:43).
* The people shared what they had with those in need (2:44–45).
* They broke bread together (2:46).
* They learned together (2:46).
* They worshipped God fervently (2:47).

The work of the Holy Spirit did not end soon after the day of Pentecost; it has continued throughout the history of the church. There is evidence that the Spirit has been at work in history regardless of the official theological positions of the church, especially regarding the charismatic aspects of life in the Spirit. This work included convicting the world of sin, bringing people to Christ, reminding believers about Jesus, empowering the church for ministry, and sanctifying the people of God (John 14:20;

16:8–11). The Spirit has sealed us (2 Cor. 1:22). He intercedes for us (Rom. 8:26) and comforts us (John 14:16 KJV). He teaches and guides us (John 14:26; 16:13; Rom. 8:14), giving us wisdom, knowledge, and liberty (1 Cor. 12:8; 2 Cor. 3:17). He has been indwelling us, helping us to resist sin (Gal. 5:17–18), and transforming us (1 John 4:13; Rom. 12:1–2).

Paul exhorted us to stir up the gifts that are within us (2 Tim. 1:6 KJV; see also 1 Thess. 5:19; 1 Tim. 4:14), and James reminded us of their Source (James 1:17). King David, Jesus, and Paul encouraged us to produce fruits (Ps. 1:3; Matt. 12:33; John 15:2, 5, 8, 16; Gal. 5:22). We must take heed.

If you are born of the Spirit and filled with the Spirit, you are a gifted person capable of manifesting both the gifts and the fruits of the Spirit. Begin to see yourself as a gifted person. He or she who has the Holy Spirit has the ultimate gift. The real gift is more than the manifestations/gifts. The fruits of the Spirit are equally vital. When I consider the instruction to walk in step with the Spirit, I think of the gifts and fruits of the Spirit as two spiritual legs that allow us to walk in the Spirit. The work of the Holy Spirit is truly profound. As a gifted person, endeavor to walk in the power of the Holy Spirit.

Be filled with the Spirit (Eph. 5:18).

Be led by the Spirit (Rom. 8:14; Gal. 5:18).

Walk in step with the Spirit (Gal. 5:25).

And as you go, fan into flame the gift of God within you (2 Tim. 1:6)!

Questions for Reflection

1. List several names and symbols of the Holy Spirit in the Bible.

2. List several places where you encounter the Spirit of God in the Old Testament.

3. Discuss the main function(s) of the Holy Spirit in the Old Testament.

4. Describe the presence of the Holy Spirit in the life and ministry of Jesus.

5. What are the main things we learn about the life and work of the Holy Spirit in the early church and in Luke's writings?

6. What major instructions regarding the Holy Spirit do we receive from the apostle Paul?

7. List and describe the gifts (comprehensive list) and fruits of the Spirit.

8. Compare and contrast these concepts: (1) being filled with the Spirit, (2) being full of the Spirit, and (3) walking in step with the Spirit.

9. Describe your personal relationship with the Holy Spirit.

10. What is the Holy Spirit saying to you about your walk with Him?

Chapter 13

You Are a Blessed Person

Bless those who persecute you;
bless and do not curse.

—ROMANS 12:14

The concept of blessing begins in the first book of the Bible. The idea of blessing in the Bible contains both the power of the words spoken as blessing and their effect. Throughout the Bible we see the dual concepts of blessing God and being blessed by God. "Blessed be God" is an expression of praise and gratitude for blessings received from God. At the same time "being blessed" refers to the reception of God's blessings by human beings. The biblical doxologies demonstrate our blessing of God. The word *doxology* is made up of two words: *doxa*, meaning "glory," and *logos*, meaning "utterance." *Doxology*, then, means pronouncing God's glory. Consider the seven doxologies from the New Testament I have listed here. Notice the dimensions of God's glory expressed in these blessings and the reasons for declaring them.

1. For new birth: "Blessed be the God and Father of our Lord Jesus Christ, who according to His abundant mercy has begotten us again to a living hope through the resurrection of Jesus Christ from the dead, to an inheritance incorruptible and undefiled and that does not fade away, reserved in heaven for you, who are kept by the power of God through faith for salvation ready to be revealed in the last time" (1 Peter 1:3–5 NKJV).

2. For making us kings and priests: "To Him who loved us and washed us from our sins in His own blood, and has made us kings and priests to His God and Father, to Him be glory and dominion forever and ever. Amen" (Rev. 1:5–6 NKJV).

3. For spiritual blessings: "Blessed *be* the God and Father of our Lord Jesus Christ, who has blessed us with every spiritual blessing in the heavenly places in Christ, just as He chose us in Him before the foundation of the world, that we should be holy and without blame before Him in love, having predestined us to adoption as sons by Jesus Christ to Himself, according to the good pleasure of His will, to the praise of the glory of His grace, by which He made us accepted in the Beloved" (Eph. 1:3–5 NKJV).

4. For care received and given: "Blessed be the God and Father of our Lord Jesus Christ, the Father of mercies and God of all comfort, who comforts us in all our tribulation, that we may be able to comfort those who are in any trouble, with the comfort with which we ourselves are comforted by God" (2 Cor. 1:3–4 NKJV).

5. For the mystery of the gospel: "Now to Him who is able to establish you according to my gospel and the preaching of Jesus Christ, according to the revelation of the mystery kept secret since the world began but now made manifest, and by the prophetic Scriptures made known to all nations, according to the commandment of the everlasting God, for obedience to the faith—to God, alone wise, be glory through Jesus Christ forever. Amen" (Rom. 16:25–27 NKJV).

6. For God's enabling power: "Now to Him who is able to do exceedingly abundantly above all that we ask or think, according to the power that works in us, to Him be glory in the church by Christ Jesus to all generations, forever and ever. Amen" (Eph. 3:20–21 NKJV).

7. For God's sustaining power: "Now to Him who is able to keep you from stumbling, and to present you faultless before the presence of His glory with exceeding joy, To God our Savior, Who alone is wise, be glory and majesty, dominion and power, both now and forever. Amen" (Jude 24–25 NKJV).

In both Testaments of the Bible, as mentioned earlier, the concept of blessing involves both the power of the words spoken and the positive effect of those words. Similarly, the idea of cursing involves the same dimensions—both power and effect—but in the most negative sense. When someone pronounces a blessing, one is pronouncing it on behalf of God. In the Bible, it is God who is the source of all blessings. We simply pronounce His blessings upon others, but the authority and power of blessings come from God. The words of blessing have power because they are pronounced on God's behalf. So we bless God for who he is and we bless each other on His behalf.

We bless God because He is good. We are able to impart blessings upon others because of our relationship with this good God. "Blessed be God" is the most common form of blessing in the Old Testament. Often this blessing is pronounced in response to some benefit received from God. "Blessed is the man" is a frequent form of biblical blessing in terms of human beings receiving God's blessings (KJV). "Blessed is" also contains the idea of being happy. "Blessed is the man" means "happy is the man." God blesses His people, but the threat of curses from God can also be found in the Bible, although the actual incidents of God's cursing are very few. God wants to bless His people; so He blesses us and allows us to bless one another on His behalf.

Pronouncing blessings was a regular part of Israel's community life. Earlier in their history, ordinary Israelites blessed one another and their children, but later the powers of blessing became centered in prophets, priests, and kings. However, the practice of blessing among the people continued. They were considered capable of pronouncing blessings on others as well as petitioning God to bless others without formal authority.

It is not possible to curse a people who have been blessed by God. For instance, Balaam's attempt to curse Israel did not work out. In fact, just the opposite happened: "However, the LORD your God would not listen to Balaam but turned the curse into a blessing for you, because the LORD your God loves you" (Deut. 23:5). One of the most beautiful Old Testament blessings is found in the book of Numbers: "The LORD bless you and keep you; the LORD make his face shine on you and be gracious to you; the LORD turn his face toward you and give you peace" (Num. 6:24–26).

The Bible teaches that God's intervention can break the hold of any curse on an individual or the community of faith (Gal. 3:13; Eph. 1:3). No power of the enemy could stand before the power of God's blessing, protection, and favor. The most destructive curse that fell on humanity is the curse of sin. Jesus Christ came to set us free from this curse. How? Paul wrote that "Christ redeemed us from the curse of the law by becoming a curse for us, for it is written: 'Cursed is everyone who is hung on a pole'" (Gal. 3:13). We have been given a choice: the choice between life and death, and blessing and curse. By faith we must choose life (Deut. 30:19) and blessing. We not only must choose blessings for ourselves, but also choose the capacity to pronounce blessings upon others in the name of our mighty God.

The people of Israel blessed God on various occasions. For instance, they blessed Him before and after their meals each day. The early Christian community adapted the Jewish custom of blessing. The Beatitudes in the Gospels introduced a new set of blessings for the followers of Jesus. Paul's letters began and concluded with blessings and benedictions.

The New Testament does not say much about curses, but we are taught that we ought to bless even those who curse us. Jesus faced the ultimate curse of sin on the cross and set us free from its effect. Now through Christ the blessings of God have come upon the circumcised and the uncircumcised alike. God's desire to bless the nations through Abraham has been fulfilled now through Jesus Christ and we are the beneficiaries. Jesus Christ is the ultimate blessing pronounced by God upon humankind. His life confers God's blessings upon us and on all those who will put their trust in Him now and in the future.

We must receive God's blessings of salvation and eternal life and bless His name in return. We must also be willing to confer God's blessings on others in the name of Jesus Christ. The power of blessing should not be ignored.

When I think of the idea of blessing others, I often think of a doctor of ministry student I knew at Oral Roberts University many years ago. I'll call him Robert. He was a fifty-five-year-old ordained minister of a major denomination. Robert was having a tough time finishing his doctor of ministry thesis. He just could not write the main part of the thesis; it was more than "writer's block." I listened to Robert as he tried to explain why he thought he could not produce the work. To my surprise he said that he was haunted by his second-grade teacher's voice, speaking to him in a very angry tone: "You are stupid, Robert. You will amount to nothing!"

That episode had occurred four decades in his past, but the words remained a loud echo in the adult Robert's mind, even after he had earned his bachelor's and master's degrees, and it still resounded as he was nearing completion of his doctorate. The truth is that Robert was a very intelligent person. He had been a successful pastor and leader, and a capable preacher of the Word of God. But deep in his heart, his wounds from the second grade remained, fighting against a greater achievement.

Our words have power, especially when we are in a position of authority, such as a teacher, pastor, or counselor. Our words impact ourselves and others in very profound ways.

As Christians, we believe that God made everything from nothing by the power of His Word. Because He made us in His own image, one of the ways that we resemble Him is that we have verbal ability not found in animals. Why should we be surprised, then, that in spite of the fall, our words carry power, especially when we speak on God's behalf?

Unfortunately, some Bible teachers have made Christians afraid to even express a need or a problem because of a fear that in so doing, they may be expressing a lack of faith. I am certainly not saying that our ordinary words are more powerful than God's Word. Yet our words do have power to impact both positively and negatively and to impart life and death. We must choose our words with discernment, especially at crucial moments in someone else's life. We must take the words of the apostle James seriously concerning the power of the tongue and do all we can to turn it into a tool of positive impact (James 3:2–6).

Psychologists have already established the value of positive self-talk. People who speak positively to themselves live better lives. Negative self-talk has the opposite effect. Words can encourage as well as discourage, empower as well as disempower, bless as well as curse. Why not use our words to encourage, empower, and bless?

The power of blessing and cursing is made very clear in the Bible. There are plenty of illustrations of both. We read that God blessed Adam, Noah, and Abraham. Abraham in turn blessed his son Isaac. Isaac then blessed his son Jacob, albeit through a switch (see Gen. 27). Jacob's history shows that even a blessing received in deception carries its power. Later on, Jacob blessed Joseph, his other sons, and his grandsons.

The story of the people of Israel is the story of a blessed people. Even when they were disobedient, the blessings seemed to provide them some protection. Jacob's struggle with the angel of the Lord by the river Jabbok and the blessing he received with "signs following" (limping) is described in detail in Genesis 32. The writer of Genesis wanted to make sure that the world understood that the people of Israel represented the sons and daughters of a blessed man, a man blessed both by God and man. Since he had deceived his father to gain his blessing, Jacob had to become brutally honest to be blessed by God. Ironically, as a man who wrestled with God to receive His blessing, Jacob later recognized God's face on his brother Esau's face (Gen. 33:10). God's blessings impact us in unpredictable and unforeseen ways.

The Bible records many other stories of blessings. Moses and Aaron as leaders blessed the people of Israel. The priests were specifically instructed to bless the people with these words: "The LORD bless you and keep you; the LORD make his face shine upon you and be gracious to you; the LORD turn his face toward you and give you peace" (Num. 6:24–26). Following the same tradition, David also blessed his people.

The history of blessings continues throughout the Bible. Although the story of the curse runs parallel to it, the blessing ultimately triumphs. God's blessings overcome the curse in all its forms.

The power of blessing is also very clearly illustrated in the New Testament. Jesus blessed the little children (Mark 10:16). According to Luke, the last act Jesus performed before his ascension was blessing: He lifted up his hands and blessed the disciples (Luke 24:50). Jesus came to bless the world with the good news. The blessing of the gospel came to us through His blessed disciples. We are now blessed and are called to bless others.

Unfortunately, we often do not bless others. We are eager to express our disapproval rather than our approval. We find ourselves cursing others instead of blessing them. It takes no more energy to bless than to curse; why, then, do we not bless? Why do we not verbally bless the ones we really want to see blessed?

This is a vital concept in parenting. All of us want our children blessed; yet how often do we bless them? Why do we let minor irritations prevent us from blessing our offspring? I believe we must look for opportunities to bless our children. Let them hear us blessing them. Let them remember our blessings. When they go out to face the world on their own, let them find strength and courage in the memory of the blessings we have pronounced over them. This thought alone must cause us to bless them, even if there were no other mysteries in the act of blessing!

We must bless others also, including our family members and friends. Teachers must bless their students. Pastors, like the Old Testament priests, must bless their people. Church services should not be concluded without a benediction. Supervisors should bless their associates, and why not? Current secular books on corporate leadership are encouraging positive reinforcement of workers with encouraging and uplifting words. Blessing may be the most cost-effective employee benefit!

Suppose Pastor Robert's second-grade teacher, instead of cursing him with a negative opinion four decades ago, had said to the boy, "Robert, I bless you in the name of God. You are a blessed child. God will help you with your studies, and you will be a success. Remember, Robert: with God's help, you may even earn a doctorate someday!" Instead of cursing, that teacher could have planted a good seed of blessing in his life, using the same time and energy it took to curse him. Then he would not have been still haunted by those wounding words in his middle age. Instead, he would have remembered her with the fondest of memories and gratitude.

Thank God for the redeeming and healing power of the Holy Spirit. Robert did receive his healing from the wounds of second grade, and he was able to complete his thesis and receive his doctorate. Focused prayers and encouragement from his professors ministered to Robert. Today he is a powerful minister of the gospel; he is busy ministering to others who have also been wounded by careless words. With the help of the Holy Spirit, Robert finally found a way to break out of the memory of the old curse, and began to give blessings to others.

You are blessed by God, and you carry the power to bless others. Claim that power and bless others in the name of our Lord and Savior Jesus Christ. This is in keeping with the best traditions of our Jewish and Christian heritage.

Questions for Reflection

1. Explain the following two concepts: "Blessed be God" and "Blessed is the man . . ."
2. What are the major aspects of a blessing and the source of power behind it?
3. What are your thoughts on the seven doxologies mentioned in this chapter?
4. What does the Bible teach about blessings and curses?
5. What are the prescribed words of the blessing pronounced by the Jewish priest?
6. What do we learn from Balaam's attempt to curse Israel?
7. What does this chapter say about Jacob wrestling with God to receive His blessing?
8. What did Jesus do with the curse of death that was on us? How?
9. What are the lessons from Robert's story?
10. What resolutions would you make regarding blessing and cursing?

Chapter 14

You Are a Saint, Now

*All the saints greet you, but especially
those who are of Caesar's household.*

—PHILIPPIANS 4:22 NKJV

I was sad to read the Barna Research Group's study of Christians
that said that Christians in America are living just like non-
Christians (see chapter 4). That study included evangelicals and
people who claim to be Spirit-filled.

The time in which we live is called the *postmodern age*.
Europeans call this the post-Christian period. Some call this
the New Age. We have a new generation that thinks differently
about spiritual matters than their parents' generation did. Two
grand ideas are very important to this group. The first idea
is "tolerance." They believe that all lifestyles must be equally

respected and tolerated without judgment. The second idea concerns spirituality. This generation believes that, generally speaking, all religions are basically equal and all sacred texts are equally inspired and reliable and deserving of the same degree of authority. Organized religion generally is bad, they believe, but "spirituality," on the other hand, is to be highly desired.

I have asked seminary students to define Spirit-filled spirituality or Spirit-empowered piety. Often they could not define these terms. I would like to look at this question in this chapter. How would you define Spirit-empowered spirituality?

We know that different religions and faith groups express their spiritualities differently. It is important that we see spirituality as exercised by different religions and compare them to Christian spirituality, and particularly Spirit-empowered spirituality.

Let's begin with Hindu spirituality and spiritual practices. Hindu spirituality, developed and cultivated in India, includes repetition of mantras, religious yoga, *pujas* or ceremonial invocations, dietary practices, and worship of the sun, moon, stars, air, earth, water, birds, fish, and the fearful forces of nature. Buddhist spiritual practices, also rooted in India's history and culture and developed in other parts of Asia, include meditation to empty the self, repetition of regimented prayers, the writing of poetry called haiku, tea ceremonies, painting, and maintenance of Zen gardens.

Muslim spirituality and spiritual practices are built on the five pillars of Islam: (1) *Shahada*, or profession of faith; (2) *Salat*, or ritual washing and prayer; (3) *Zakat*, or almsgiving; (4)

Sawm, or fasting during Ramadan; and (5) *Hajj*, or pilgrimage to Mecca. Jewish spirituality, on the other hand, is distinctive and is built around the Torah. It emphasizes the Sabbath, proper diet, ethical living, and celebrating feasts such as the Passover and Hanukkah.

When it comes to Christian spirituality, Catholic spirituality expresses itself in confessions, attending the mass, prayers, prescribed fasting, self-sacrifices, and participation in various sacraments and rituals. Orthodox spirituality has many similarities with Catholic expressions in spite of the theological differences. Generally speaking, Protestant spirituality is expressed in regular worship, Bible study, fasting and prayer, devotional reading, evangelism, and participation in the ordinances of the church.

What about Spirit-filled spirituality? Is it just loud singing, modern music, or speaking in tongues? Having mist and laser beams in the darkened sanctuary? Or not having a printed order of worship? I believe theologian Steve Land is right when he says that Spirit-filled or Pentecostal spirituality has three dimensions: *thinking, feeling, and doing.*[24] *Thinking* has to do with the question, "What do you believe?" *Feelings* have to do with our religious affections, dealing with the question, "What are our feelings?" The affections have to do with where one's heart is. And *doing* deals with the question, "What are your actual spiritual practices, actions, and habits?" In other words, *thinking* has to do with doctrines, *feelings* have to do with our deep commitments, and *doing* has to do with our practices.

---

24 Steven Land, *Pentecostal Spirituality: A Passion for the Kingdom* (Sheffield, England: Sheffield Academic Press, 1994), 41.

A healthy Spirit-empowered spirituality must deal with the right doctrines.

A healthy Spirit-empowered spirituality must deal with the right affections.

A healthy Spirit-empowered spirituality must deal with the right spiritual practices.

Right Doctrines. Having the right doctrines means having a correct theology. Unfortunately, in some circles, *theology* is a dirty word. This is a mistaken notion. Theology is not a dirty word, because it simply means "study of God." Everyone has a theology; it may be good or bad. Theology does matter. When I was a chaplain many years ago, a medical doctor reminded me that bad medicine kills, but so does bad theology. Theology is not the problem; bad theology is. We need good theology. We need good doctrines. We must learn from the Bereans in the book of Acts: "Now the Berean Jews were of more noble character than those in Thessalonica, for they received the message with great eagerness and examined the Scriptures every day to see if what Paul said was true" (Acts 17:11).

What are the basic doctrines of people who consider themselves Spirit-empowered? Here's the simplest way we can summarize the answer: We believe in the life, death, and resurrection of Jesus, His ascension, and His promise of second coming. Everything we believe is based on this sentence. Salvation is based on the life, death, and resurrection of Jesus. Baptism in water, baptism in the Holy Spirit, sanctified life, signs and wonders, healing, evangelism, and our ultimate hope of resurrection are based on this idea of the life, death, and resurrection of Jesus.

Right Affections. What are the Spirit-filled affections? Healthy spirituality has emotions and must deal with them. Right affections mean right emotions. Steve Land says that there are three major affections in the life of a Spirit-filled person: (1) compassion, (2) courage, (3) and gratitude.[25] Compassion for the needy, courage to go where God's light is seen dimly, and gratitude expressed to God in worship are the basic affections of a Spirit-filled Christian. Land believes that all these are tied up with the idea of the kingdom of God.

Right Practices. When it comes to the best practices related to Spirit-empowered spirituality, the Bible gives many lists of right practices. For example, Acts 2 gives this list: studying the apostles' doctrines, fellowship, breaking of bread, prayers, joyful worship, signs and wonders, sharing of possessions, and sharing of faith with others (vv. 42–27). Paul the apostle gives us several similar lists. One list is found in 1 Thessalonians 5: (1) rejoice always, (2) pray continually, (3) give thanks in all circumstances, and (4) do not quench the Spirit, (5) do not treat prophecies with contempt but test them all, (6) hold on to what is good, (7) reject every kind of evil (vv. 16–19). In other words, we are to be joyful, prayerful, thankful, and Spirit-empowered.

These lists are helpful, but Spirit-empowered spirituality cannot be limited to some lists of do's and don'ts. Fulfilling a list is not what God expects of us. Conforming to certain external regulations is not the way we maintain true Spirit-filled spirituality. Spiritual practices for Spirit-filled people must be expressions

---

25 Land, 138.

of the work of the Holy Spirit inside them. They are expressions of Spirit-led, Spirit-empowered, and transformed lives.

Some of us grew up with long lists of do's and don'ts. We were proud of the things we did not do. In fact, our list had more don'ts than do's. Unfortunately, the list of sins kept growing and changing. Hopefully, we have learned much from those days and are looking at spirituality in a more mature and comprehensive way now.

Let me tell you what this means to me. We must live transformed lives. The Bible tells us that we have been instantly changed, but not instantly matured. We do not become spiritual giants in one day, but we are changed in one day. Some Christians seem to be waiting to be changed after their death, but the Bible talks about change taking place here and now. And it commands transformation now: "Do not conform to the pattern of this world, but be transformed by the renewing of your mind. Then you will be able to test and approve what God's will is—his good, pleasing and perfect will" (Rom. 12:2). We have been born again by being born of the Spirit of God. Additionally, we have been filled with the Spirit. Our spirituality must become an expression of this truth—an expression of the transformed life that we live by faith *today*. We are not perfect, but we are transformed. We have been changed.[26]

Paul's writings describe our present life as he saw it. According to Paul, we are accepted by God (Eph. 1:6); we are adopted by

---

[26] I wish to acknowledge the information and inspiration I received on this concept from the seven volumes of the Pursuing with Passion Series authored by Chaplain J. W. Phillips.

God (Eph. 1:5); we are God's workmanship (Eph. 2:10). We are forgiven; we are sealed by the Holy Spirit (Eph. 1:13); we are rich in inheritance (Col. 1:12). We are citizens of God's kingdom (Phil. 3:20); we belong to the household of faith (Eph. 2:19). We have been crucified with Christ (Gal. 2:20) and raised up (Eph. 2:6). We have become a new creation! (2 Cor. 5:17) The same writings discuss our future also. It is a pleasant surprise to discover that our present is meant to be very much like our future and our future is meant to be very much like our present.

According to Paul, Christ is seated at the right hand of God and we are seated with Him now. We live in Him here and now. We are rooted in Him and hidden in Him. We are children of God now. Not through a biological heritage, like the Jews, nor by our religious performances. We have been grafted to the vine to draw from God's nature. We are in a connected position to receive the life and nature of God now. God initiated this process and provides everything we need to sustain it. This is Spirit-filled spirituality. This is Spirit-empowered spirituality (Eph. 2:6; Gal. 2:20; Col. 3:3; Gal. 3:14).

The idea is simple. We are God's children. The holy God is our Father. We have inherited His nature in us as we have been born of the Spirit and have been filled with the Spirit. We see the offspring of all creatures inheriting the nature of their parents. We see all creatures displaying the characteristics of their progenitors. They naturally express the characteristics of their DNA. We cannot ignore the fact that God's children have His nature in them even as they live in this fallen world. This is why we are called saints.

The fullness of our inheritance has not been realized, but we are saved by faith, by the grace of God. We are saved indeed. Those who are saved are called saints in the Bible. And we are saints now—living saints. Many somehow still maintain the idea that all saints are dead people whose statues are kept in religious places. No, not all saints are dead and gone. We who are saved by grace and are filled with the Holy Spirit are living saints. We are so by faith. Yes, we are saints, now.

We had an old nature, and it was not pleasing to God. Our old righteousness was like filthy rags (Isa. 64:6). We were not in a position to save ourselves, but God saved us and made us a new creation in Jesus Christ. We have been made anew. We are born of God, born of His Spirit, and brought to life in Jesus Christ. Our life is now hidden in God with Christ (Col. 3:3). No wonder Paul found saints even in Caesar's palace!

We have been set free from the bondage of sin. We have been changed and transformed. We are now God's workmanship, His masterpieces. This is a profound and liberating truth, especially for those of us who grew up in legalism. Many of our churches and ministries are performance-based. It is time to release ourselves from the bondage of legalism and claim the freedom that God has given us. Let us express that freedom in our spirituality by allowing the nature of God that is in us to display itself by grace, empowered and guided by the Holy Spirit.

The enemy of our soul does not want us to think this way, feel this way, or believe this way. He wants us to live as if we have not changed. He wants us to live as if spirituality is some kind of legalistic exercise filled with condemnation. He wants us to live in fear of falling down all the time. But that's not what the Word of God tells us. We can depend on the power of the Holy Spirit and live out true Spirit-empowered spirituality by the grace of God. It is time to live this out. It is time to live this out by faith.

We are not claiming that we are now perfect and without any faults. We are not saying that we have been released from holy living and spiritual accountability. On the contrary, we recognize that as wholeness is a dynamic status by faith, so is holiness. Wholeness is by faith. So also is holiness. Actually, Oral Roberts was right: wholeness is holiness. We will mature gradually, but we will live in God-granted holiness now. We have been changed already, although we are not complete yet. We have not yet been fully transformed, but we shall be. Meanwhile, God's Spirit has given us a new birth, which has given us a new nature. As we continue to mature as children of God, our transformed life is increasingly being revealed and expressed. Our spiritual DNA is taking expression and manifesting in our practices. This is true Spirit-filled spirituality.

This means we don't have to feel helpless and hopeless anymore in terms of our lifestyle. We can live a whole-person life. We can keep a whole-person lifestyle. Not by might, nor by power, but by God's Spirit (Zech. 4:6). We are free now. Freedom is ours through Jesus Christ now. We no longer have to live in bondage. We have been crucified with Christ, but live now as new creations in the newness of life. We live by faith in the Son of God, who loved us and gave himself for us (Eph. 5:2). We are each a new creation in Him (2 Cor. 5:17). We are called saints now (1 Cor. 1:2 KJV).

You are born of the Spirit and filled with the Spirit. You have been sanctified by the Word (Acts 20:32), the Spirit (Rom. 15:16), and the blood of Jesus Christ (Heb. 10:29). Release the Spirit of holiness within you by faith. You are sealed by the Holy Spirit (Eph. 4:30), and the deposit of the Spirit is in you already (2 Cor. 1:22). The Spirit that raised Jesus from the dead dwells in you now (Rom. 8:11). That same Spirit has transformed you and is transforming you; that same Spirit will transform your mortal body and raise you up from the dead someday. This process will fully mature you in due time, but you don't have to wait for full maturity to express your new spirituality. Believe the Word of God, keep the right affections, release the Spirit of holiness within you, and walk by faith. You have already left the kingdom of darkness. You are in the kingdom of light now. The Holy Spirit has made this possible. You can live a holy and victorious Christian life by the power of the Holy Spirit. Yes, you are a saint, now.

Questions for Reflection

1. Comment on the Barna Group research mentioned in this chapter (see also chapter 4).
2. What are the two major values of the postmodern generation? Critique.
3. Comment on the major practices of spirituality among Hindus, Buddhists, Muslims, and Jews.
4. Comment on the different emphases in Catholic, Orthodox, and Protestant traditions of Christianity.
5. What are the three dimensions of Spirit-empowered spirituality, according to Steve Land?
6. Define *doctrines*, *affections*, and *spiritual practices* with respect to Spirit-empowered Christians.
7. Describe Paul's view of our present and future based on the epistles to the Ephesians and Colossians.
8. Discuss these concepts: holiness, maturity, discipline, and accountability.
9. What is the definition of a saint in the Bible?
10. Defend the statement: "You are a saint, now."

Chapter 15

You Are an Anointed Person,
Empowered to Fulfill Your Purpose

*Then Samuel took a flask of oil and poured
it on his head, and kissed him and said:
"Is it not because the LORD has anointed
you commander over His inheritance?"*

—1 SAMUEL 10:1

The concept called "paradigm shift" entered our everyday vocabulary during the last part of the twentieth century. Thomas Kuhn, an American philosopher of science, is credited with the coining of this term. When the usual way of thinking about and doing something is replaced with a fundamentally and significantly different way, it is called a paradigm shift.

Examples abound. There was a time, for instance, when watches were made with mechanical springs. Electronic and digital watches have replaced them. This is considered a paradigm shift. A similar change happened in the way we take photos. Our cameras have been replaced by our cell phones and the younger generation has no idea what a Kodak film or Polaroid camera looked like. The underground oil pipes that used to make big profits in the past for oil companies in Oklahoma are now making profits for new corporations by moving information through them, instead of oil, with the help of fiber optic cables. These are paradigm shifts.

The book of 1 Samuel presents a tall and handsome young man named Saul who needed a paradigm shift in the way he thought about himself. When we find him in chapter 9, he is chasing his father's lost donkeys. Here is a young man who was meant to be the first king of Israel, spending his days looking for his father's donkeys. It looks like his family had no grasp of what God had in store for young Saul, and he seemed to have even less. In fact, from his conversation with the prophet Samuel, it is clear that he was not just humble, but had a poor self-concept based on his family of origin (1 Sam. 9:21).

Samuel asked him to stop for a moment to share with him God's plan for his life. Saul sent his servant away and spent time with the prophet. As he left, Samuel anointed him with oil and told him God's plan for his life. He would be king of Israel! He could not believe it. Saul left in shock.

The truth is that we are very much like Saul. We are busy chasing donkeys, often based on what others have told us about us and our future. The donkeys have changed their looks since Saul's days. Now they take the form of a car, a house, a job, a mortgage, leisure, the Internet, multimedia, entertainment, and so on.

We must recognize our true identity and realize that we are more than donkey chasers. We are the Lord's anointed, God's beloved people, washed in the blood of Jesus, and called to be a kingdom, a priesthood, and a chosen people. We have been called for a purpose. Listen to John: "To him who loves us and has freed us from our sins by his blood, and has made us to be a kingdom and priests to serve his God and Father—to him be glory and power for ever and ever! Amen" (Rev. 1:5–6). Say amen to Peter: "But you are a chosen people, a royal priesthood, a holy nation, God's special possession, that you may declare the praises of him who called you out of darkness into his wonderful light" (1 Peter 2:9).

Worries and fears cause us to chase donkeys. The sad thing is that some of our fears are truly groundless. I was once a chaplain trainee at Norwich Hospital in Norwich, Connecticut. One day I was driving from New Haven to Norwich in my green Plymouth Barracuda. The sun was shining when I left New Haven, but the weather drastically changed midway. Ice and snow seemed to come down together, and the road became extremely slippery. Having come from tropical India, I had no experience in driving in ice and snow at that time. I was having trouble controlling my car, and finally I slid to the edge of the highway and stayed where the car stopped. Visibility was very poor, and no one else was on the road, and I panicked.

I looked for a road sign to see where I was. Seeing a blue sign at a distance, I strained to read it, only to be shocked as I read, "Panic Area!" My panic increased. I could not believe that I had wound up in such a place. Once I got my bearing, I decided to read the blue sign again, only to find out that it actually read, "Picnic Area!"

How often do we panic in picnic areas! These panics, along with other people's expectations of us, cause us to miss God's plans and purposes for our lives, which are bigger than our calculations. In Saul's case, he was actually chasing donkeys that had already been found. He needed to hear God's voice. What he really needed was a life-transforming encounter with God's word.

We have already seen that an encounter with God can transform us. There are so many to testify to this truth. An encounter with God changed Abraham's destiny (Gen. 17:1–6). An encounter with God molded Jacob (Gen. 32:26). Moses was transformed by an encounter with the living God (Ex. 3:1–7). Joshua was also transformed (Josh. 1:1–5). Samuel was never the same again after his encounter with God's call (1 Sam. 3:4ff). Elijah and Ezekiel were changed by God's voice (1 Kings 17:2–3ff; Eze. 1:1).

I draw two important lessons from Saul's experience of chasing donkeys:

1. We must live in the awareness of God's presence.
2. We must live to fulfill God's purpose for our lives.

Living in the awareness of God's presence and focusing on fulfilling His plans for our lives will help us fight our poor self-concepts and reach the full potential of our lives. Instead of fulfilling other people's expectations of us, we will discover our purpose in God's heart and fulfill His dream for us.

Living in the awareness of God's presence. The Bible is a record of God's dealings with human beings, so the presence of God is a continuous theme in both Old and New Testaments. Here's a brief survey.

The presence of God in the garden. Naked and ashamed, Adam hid behind the trees in the garden, and God showed up in the garden looking for him. This is where Christian faith departs from all others. While other religions point the way to God and ask man to take the road, the Christian faith talks about a God who is in search of hurting humans. God brought His presence to the lost souls in the garden of Eden.

The presence of God in the wilderness. "By day the LORD went ahead of them in a pillar of cloud to guide them on their way and by night in a pillar of fire to give them light, so that they could travel by day or night" (Ex. 13:21). God's people were leaving the bondage of Egypt. After witnessing the amazing signs and wonders that gave them freedom, they were traveling through the treacherous desert. The heat of the day was harsh and the cold of the night was unbearable. Men, women, and children were trekking through the desert, facing the dangers of the wilderness each day and every night. Guess where God was at that time. He was going before them as a pillar of cloud by day and as a pillar of fire by night. His presence was with His people during their painful journey.

The presence of God in the temple. When the people of Israel arrived in the Promised Land, God blessed them and prospered them. One day He told Solomon, "As for this temple you are building, if you follow my decrees, observe my laws and keep all my commands and obey them, I will fulfill through you the promise I gave to David your father. And I will live among the Israelites and will not abandon my people Israel" (1 Kings 6:12–13). It took thirty thousand men working for seven years to complete the temple. A single shift had ten thousand men. The temple was completed in 960 BC. Look what happened at the dedication of the temple.

> When Solomon finished praying, fire came down from heaven and consumed the burnt offering and the sacrifices, and the glory of the LORD filled the temple. The priests could not enter the temple of the LORD because the glory of the LORD filled it. When all the Israelites saw the fire coming down and the glory of the LORD above the temple, they knelt on the pavement with their faces to the ground, and they worshiped and gave thanks to the LORD, saying, "He is good; his love endures forever." (2 Chron. 7:1–3)

God never abandoned His people. His presence remained with them, even when they were disobedient.

Solomon's temple was destroyed by the Babylonians in 586 BC. It was rebuilt by Zerubbabel after fifty + years, and it was finished in 516 BC. This temple was replaced later by Herod's, which remained open from 20 BC to AD 70.

Something fantastic happened during this period. Let's listen to John:

> In the beginning was the Word, and the Word was with God, and the Word was God. . . . The Word became flesh and made his dwelling among us. We have seen his glory, the glory of the one and only Son, who came from the Father, full of grace and truth. (John 1:1, 14)

Hear Matthew:

> "The virgin will conceive and give birth to a son, and they will call him Immanuel" (which means "God with us"). (Matt. 1:23)

Now listen to Paul:

> God was in Christ, reconciling the world unto himself, not imputing their trespasses unto them; and hath committed unto us the word of reconciliation. (2 Cor. 5:19 KJV)

> For in Christ all the fullness of the Deity lives in bodily form. (Col. 2:9)

Not in scores of religious leaders, but in Christ alone.

Here's the scandalous claim: God became man and lived among us. In the language of *The Message* Bible, "The Word became flesh and blood, and moved into the neighborhood" (John 1:14 MSG). Meditate on this. *Jehovah*, the Eternal One, became flesh. *El Shaddai*, the all-sufficient God, became flesh. *Jehovah-jireh*, our Provider, became flesh. *Jehovah-Rapha*, our Healer, became flesh and lived among us. Yes, the Immanuel—God with us—came.

Jesus Christ was the presence of God on planet Earth for thirty-three years. He went around doing good, preaching, teaching, and healing, and His disciples saw His glory (John 1:14). But He was nailed to a cross by those who could not handle pure holiness. He died between two thieves, was buried, but rose again on the third day and ascended to His Father. What happened to the presence of God then?

Pentecost came as the presence of God on planet Earth. Luke tells us about the day of Pentecost:

> Suddenly a sound like the blowing of a violent wind came from heaven and filled the whole house where they were sitting. They saw what seemed to be tongues of fire that separated and came to rest on each of them. All of them were filled with the Holy Spirit and began to speak in other tongues as the Spirit enabled them. (Acts 2:2–4)

Jesus, as He had promised earlier, sent His dynamic presence through the Holy Spirit to the upper room where those awaiting the promise were gathered. The presence of God came like a mighty rushing wind, and it blew across the world from Jerusalem, to Caesarea, to Ephesus, to Rome, and to the uttermost bounds of the earth. It was like a river flowing from heaven, running through Jerusalem, and flowing to the ends of the earth.

In terms of recent history, Topeka, Houston, and Los Angeles in the United States, and cities and towns in Norway, Sweden, and all the way to Far East India were impacted by this river. The wind blew at its pleasure, and the presence of God in the power of the Holy Spirit was felt across the world. The wind has not stopped blowing. Hundreds of millions of people on planet Earth bear witness to this experience now.

The church represents the presence of God now. "For where two or three gather in my name, there am I with them," Jesus said (Matt. 18:20). Paul clarified it after the day of Pentecost: "Don't you know that you yourselves are God's temple and that God's Spirit dwells in your midst?" (1 Cor. 3:16). He tells us that we who are many are one temple where God's presence is. The presence of Jesus in the power of the Holy Spirit manifests as we gather in His name. The church is the called and gathered people of God. God's presence is in the midst of the church, bearing witness to Jesus, and saving, healing, teaching, and sanctifying His people.

God's presence is with and within the individual believer. When the benediction is pronounced at the end of a church gathering, the presence of God does not disappear. As we have seen in previous chapters, the presence of God indwells each

Christian and goes with him or her. We are called to be filled with the Spirit. We are admonished to walk in the Spirit. We are promised to be led by the Spirit. Theologians call it *incarnational presence*, which is defined as "Christ in you, the hope of glory" (Col. 1:27). The apostle Paul put it simply as a question: "Do you not know that your bodies are temples of the Holy Spirit, who is in you, whom you have received from God?" (1 Cor. 6:19).

Live to fulfill God's purpose. Saul was unaware of the presence of God in his life as he chased his father's donkeys. He was also unaware of his destiny to be the king of Israel. Having a king of their own was a paradigm shift for Israel at that time as until then they'd had no kings. They were being led by the prophet Samuel. Saul needed a paradigm shift within a paradigm shift. He was called to fulfill God's plan for his life, which was way beyond all that he could ask or imagine. Samuel called him to his purpose and anointed him. Saul was called to live and fulfill God's purpose for his life. We must also do the same. As people called and anointed, we must live a certain way to reach our full potential.

Pastor Rick Warren's well-known book *The Purpose Driven Life* proposed five specific purposes of God for His children:[27]

1. We must please God because we are planned for God's pleasure.

---

27 Rick Warren, *The Purpose Filled Life: What on Earth Am I Here For?*, expanded ed. (Grand Rapids: Zondervan, 2012).

2. We are to belong to God's family because we are formed to be part of His family.

3. We are purposed to be like Christ because we are created to be like Him.

4. We are to serve God because we are shaped to serve our Maker.

5. We must preach the good news because we are made for a mission.

I have come up with a simple three-step way to fulfill God's purpose for our lives regardless of the specifics of our calling:

* We must live by faith.
* We must walk within our calling.
* We must walk in our anointing.

We must live by faith. God's purpose for His children is that they should live by faith in Him. I consider several definitions of faith as I say this. First of all, faith is "confidence in what we hope for and assurance about what we do not see" (Heb. 11:1). Remember that faith sees the invisible, believes the incredible, and accomplishes the impossible. Looking at the life of Abraham, one can say that faith begins the journey without knowing the destination; faith waits without knowing how long the wait is; faith obeys instructions without knowing the reasons; and faith receives rewards without knowing how they are generated.

Our ultimate purpose is to please God. Faith pleases God (Heb. 11:6). In India, where I grew up, pastors' homes were called faith homes because in those days pastors lived without any definite salary or benefit packages. They lived by trusting God and depending on the freewill offerings people gave them. In other words, pastors in India *really* lived by faith in those days. I don't believe that is the case in India anymore, but I now believe that every Christian home in all parts of the world should be a faith home.

Living by faith means we are open to new possibilities and new paradigms. It means we can discern and discover God's plans and purposes more clearly. A willingness to live by faith and not by sight is the beginning of fulfilling God's purpose for our lives.

We must walk within our calling. Discovering God's call is a blessed experience. Walking within that calling is the most blessed life. I have noticed individuals wandering through life without knowing their calling, and being very miserable. These are not people in the field of ministry. I do not believe in separating the secular from the sacred in a Christian's life. We are called to do all unto Christ. That means, in God's sight, everything we do is sacred as a matter of stewardship. It does not matter if one is a researcher or a revivalist. When done for the glory of God, each one's labor becomes a God-honoring vocation.

The Bible provides abundant testimonies of people discovering their callings. God had a plan for Abraham's life. He was to become a nation to bless the nations of the world. He discovered it and responded to it by faith. God had a plan for Joseph. He had a destiny beyond the pit, Potiphar's house, and the prison. He was to preserve his family and save a nation. Moses was not to die in a tiny ark flowing down the Nile or to become a Pharaoh with a big tall pyramid to his name. His calling was to deliver his people from bondage and bring them to the Promised Land. Daniel was not to be corrupted in Babylon. He was called to influence that nation, not be defiled by it. Elijah was not to live in depression, with suicidal thoughts. His calling was to reveal the living God to the heathens. Jonah was not to drown in the sea or suffocate in the belly of a big fish. His calling was to carry the message of forgiveness to the inhabitants of Nineveh, whom he despised. Peter was not to end his career by denying Jesus in front of his enemies. He was destined to preach the powerful message of God's plan of salvation on the day of Pentecost. Paul was not going to end his life as a persecutor of God's people or die in a shipwreck on the way to Rome. His calling was to bear witness to the gospel in the Gentile world. All these men discovered God's purposes for their lives and yielded by faith. Blessed is the person who discovers God's calling and lives within that calling.

There were also plenty of women in the Bible who found their calling and lived by it. Sarah found her calling to be the mother of a nation. Deborah found her calling to be a leader of great stature. Ruth found her calling to become the ever-so-great-grandmother of Jesus. Rahab found a calling in hosting the Hebrew spies. Mary found her calling to bear the Savior of the world. Mary Magdalene found her calling to be the first evangelist. Rufus's mother and Priscilla the deaconess discovered their calling to minister in the first-century church.

I have witnessed the frustration of people who missed their calling. This includes individuals who missed their calling at an early stage and tried to overcompensate for lost time later in life, making themselves and others very miserable in the process. Discover your calling and walk in it by faith as early in life as possible.

Another observation I have made is of people who tried to walk outside or beyond their calling and causing much pain to themselves and others. I knew a man once whom God used in a profound way to minister to people in a pastoral way through a ministry of prayer and intercession. He was used at times to speak into people's lives through words of knowledge and spiritual insights. However, I watched the same person later when he called himself a prophet and spoke with a tone of authority to people with words that did not exhort, edify, or comfort. Further, that person began to advise the leader of a major organization regarding who on his staff should be fired and who should not be by claiming the power of his prophetic vision and knowledge. The leader and the organization suffered greatly under this person's influence. The fact is that the man really had a genuine calling to minister to people in a very pastoral way, but when he went outside his calling and claimed improper identity and authority, many were deeply hurt and wounded. Eventually, he lost both his real and exaggerated ministries. It is better to stay within one's calling.

We must walk in our anointing. Samuel anointed Saul with oil, symbolizing the anointing of the Holy Spirit in his life for his calling to be the king of Israel. God anoints His servants for their assignments. He commissions his servants for their service. The Holy Spirit came on Saul with power. The Bible says that Saul actually received a new heart. Often a change of heart is required for a new assignment. The new anointing brought Saul new friends. It is interesting to note that these new friends were prophets. Soon after, we see Saul prophesying too. The company we keep influences us. Joining liars eventually makes one a liar; joining complainers makes one a complainer; joining the prophets makes one a prophet. A new Saul emerged, and the people asked, "What is this that has happened to the son of Kish? Is Saul also among the prophets?" (1 Sam. 10:11).

It must have been a sight to see Saul prophesying on his way to the throne. I can only conclude that he discovered his calling and was walking in his anointing.

We are asked to be filled with the Spirit, be led by the Spirit, and walk in the Spirit. The anointing is not something magical. The Holy Spirit is the anointing. One must walk in the anointing of the Holy Spirit to fulfill God's purpose.

A person called by God! That is your identity. Walk in that calling. A person anointed by God! That is who you are. You must be determined to walk within your calling and under the anointing of the Holy Spirit. That is the way to peace, joy, and victory.

I must add a word about the importance of preparing for your calling. Your calling may require new knowledge and skills. Don't be afraid to gain these. I have told Bible college and seminary students to gain the specific skills needed to fulfill their calling. Training time is not lost time. I call it "runway time." An airplane must spend some time on the runway before taking off. The larger the plane, the longer the required runway time. This is not only true of formal ministry; it is also true of all God's assignments. Forty years spent in Pharaoh's palace and an additional forty years as a shepherd in the wilderness were runway time for Moses. Don't despise small beginnings or longer training periods. These are times to learn to walk in your calling and anointing.

There is no need to walk in your calling with fear. There is no need to be intimidated by those who try to discourage you. Greater is He that is in you than He that is in the world (1 John 4:4). An experience I had as a boy in India helps me remember this truth. I was on my way to school one day when I came across a snake in my path. I could only see its moving tail at first. Having heard horror stories about Indian cobras and having had a classmate die of a snakebite, I was terrified and began to call out for neighbors to help me. A neighbor came running, carrying a big stick. He tried to find the head of the snake to beat it, but to my dismay, instead of beating the snake, he started laughing. I asked him why he was laughing instead of killing the snake. He asked me to take a look at the snake's hidden head. I looked with much fear and found that its head was beaten flat; the snake could not raise its head up. Obviously, someone had gone before me, seen the snake, and hit it on its head! Unable to move, the snake was just lying there, moving only its tail. Snakes don't kill with their tails. I was not in any danger, in spite of the terror I felt.

I see this experience as a parable now. Indeed, someone has gone before us two thousand years ago, and at a place called Calvary, He destroyed the head of the serpent. It can still try to frighten us, but its fatal power has been removed. We don't need to be afraid of the snake anymore. We should just be aware of his devices.

Discover your vocation and walk in it. Receive the anointing and power of the Holy Spirit to excel in that calling. Walk without fear. You will be walking in your true identity and fulfilling your purpose powerfully.

Questions for Reflection

1. Why was Saul chasing donkeys?
2. What was the paradigm shift Saul needed?
3. What are the lessons we learn from Saul's encounter with the prophet?
4. What was the outcome of his anointing with oil?
5. What do we know about the history of the presence of God?
6. What are the seven places of the presence of God highlighted in this chapter?
7. What are the three steps recommended in this chapter to fulfill God's purpose for your life?
8. Which of these steps do you struggle with the most?
9. What is the Lord saying to you about your identity and purpose through this chapter?
10. What plan of action might you consider taking as a first step regarding the Lord's prompting in your life?

Epilogue

Dear reader, it has been my pleasure to accompany you on this journey. In the preceding chapters, you have encountered fifteen cords or streams of your spiritual identity. These components represented three areas of concentration. The first five focused on your identity in relation to the family of God. The second group dealt with your identity in terms of God's purposes for your life, and the last group presented your identity with respect to the empowerment of the Holy Spirit. Your psychosocial identity, which considers your family, race, ethnicity, economics, and so on, is only partial. You do not disown it, but your true identity is your spiritual identity, and it is derived from your position in God's family, your purpose based on God's call, and your empowerment by the Holy Spirit.

God wants His children to know who they are in Him. He wants us to have a glimpse of how He sees us. This is an awesome revelation to most of us because for one reason or another we have a distorted view of ourselves. Input and reactions we have received from others and the lies the enemy has spoken to us have contributed to our distorted view. God's Word is the most reliable mirror to see ourselves as God sees us. He wants us to see this reflection for ourselves. I hope you had a good opportunity to look at yourself through these chapters. My prayer is that the reflection you saw was more beautiful, purposeful, and empowering than you could imagine.

As I mentioned in the introduction, distorted perceptions of ourselves are at the root of many problems and failures we experience in life. Having a more accurate perception of who we are based on the Word of God is the beginning of overcoming these issues. I am confident that when we see ourselves in relation to the family of God, the purposes of God, and the power of the Holy Spirit, we will experience a paradigm shift and begin a new way of living.

I ask you to trust the images you have seen of yourselves in these chapters. In terms of your relationship within the family of God, I ask you to see yourself as a child of God, a member of His family, a citizen of His kingdom, a disciple of Jesus Christ, and a whole person. Regarding your identity in terms of God's purposes for your life, I ask you to see yourself as a person called to be a healer who represents Jesus, the Wounded Healer. See yourself as a hope-bearer in a hopeless world, a person called to lead others, one who is called to be a missionary with a message and a prophetic voice for your generation.

Finally, in terms of empowerment, see your body as a temple of the Holy Spirit. You are an anointed person who has received *the* gift of the Holy Spirit, which contains the supernatural manifestations (gifts) of the Holy Spirit and the potential to develop all the fruits of the Spirit in your life. See yourself as a blessed person who is commissioned to bless others, as a saint with divine power and protection, and as one who lives out a calling in the awareness of the presence and power of God.

Ask the Holy Spirit to help you incorporate into your very being this multifaceted biblical view of yourself. Open your life to the work of the Holy Spirit to make this perception a vital part of your reality and worldview. By faith, begin to function with an understanding of God's perceptions of you in terms of who you are, what you are called to do, and the empowerment that is available to you. Let the threads of your true identity become a strong cord; let the streams of your spiritual identity become a mighty river in your life.

Reflect on what you have read and studied. Don't be afraid to declare your identity to yourself. Say to yourself, "I am a child of God," "I am a member of God's family," "I am a disciple of Jesus Christ," "I am a citizen of the kingdom of God," "I am a whole person," and so forth.

With an increased sensitivity, begin to see yourself as God sees you. Commit yourself to walk by faith in this identity and claim the authority it provides you. Walk in the power of the Holy Spirit as you go into your personal world, and be a whole person in this broken world. May the voice of God your "Abba," the light of His glorious presence, and His unlimited healing power accompany you into your new day. And may you walk in the revelation of who you really are and whom you serve for the rest of your journey to the celestial city.

I wish you Godspeed!

www.thomsonkmathew.com

88819580R00150

Made in the USA
Columbia, SC
05 February 2018